# LARRY SANG'S

## CHINESE ASTROLOGY & FENG SHUI GUIDE

# 2012

## *The Year of The Dragon*

with Lorraine Wilcox

# LARRY SANG'S
## *The Year of The Dragon*
## ASTROLOGY AND FENG SHUI GUIDE

Original Title:
**Master Larry Sang's 2012 The Year of the Dragon,
Astrology and Feng Shui Guide**

Published by: The American Feng Shui Institute
7220 N. Rosemead Blvd., Suite 204
San Gabriel, CA 91775
Email: fsinfo@amfengshui.com
www.amfengshui.com

Written by:
Master Larry Sang

Edited by:
Lorraine Wilcox

Cover Design & Illustration by:
Afriany Simbolon

*Live in the present,*
*don't wait until tomorrow;*
*pick your roses today*

活在當下

花開堪折直須折

莫待無花空折枝

Calligraphy by Larry Sang

# Please Read This Information

This book provides information regarding the subject matter covered. The authors are not engaged in rendering legal, medical or other professional advice. If you need medical or legal advice, a competent professional should be contacted. Chinese Astrology and Feng Shui are not get-rich-quick or cure-all schemes. Changes in your life will happen as fast as you are ready for them. Be patient in your study of Chinese Astrology and Feng Shui.

The authors have tried to make this book as complete and accurate as possible. However, there may be typographical or content mistakes. Use this book as a general guide in your study of Chinese Astrology and Feng Shui.

This book was written to educate and entertain. The authors, distributors and the American Feng Shui Institute shall have neither liability nor responsibility to any person with respect to any loss or damage caused, or alleged to be caused by this book.

The following pages of predictions will help you understand trends as they develop through the coming year. Please keep in mind that they are somewhat general because other stellar influences are operative, according to the month, date and exact minute of your birth. Unfortunately, we cannot deal with each person individually in this book.

# Table of Contents

只缺乏激情
誰以取得
偉大的成功

**Nothing great was ever achieved
without enthusiasm**

Calligraphy by Larry Sang

# How to find Your Animal Sign

In order to find your correct animal sign, as well as understand why the Chinese calendar begins in February, and not January, it is important to have a little understanding of the two different Chinese calendars. As with most things Chinese, we look at the Yin and Yang. In Chinese timekeeping, there is a Yin Calendar (Lunar calendar) and a Yang Calendar (Solar calendar).

## The Lunar Calendar

The Lunar calendar is perhaps the best known and most popular of the two. Chinese Lunar New Year is frequently celebrated with a lot of pageantry. It is used in one type of Chinese Astrology called Zi Wei Dou Shu, and also in Yi Jing calculations.

## The Solar Calendar

The Solar calendar is less well known. The early Chinese meteorologists attempts to gain insight into the cycles of the seasons. From this study, this developed the Solar calendar. This calendar is used in the form of Chinese Astrology called Four Pillars, as well as in Feng Shui. The Chinese were very accurate in their studies. Without computers, and using only observations, they mapped a solar year of 365 days. They missed the actual timing of a year by only 14 minutes and 12 seconds.

The solar year is divided into 24 solar terms. Each lasts about fifteen days. Spring Begins (lichun) is the name of the first day of Spring, and the first solar term. It is exactly midway between the winder solstice and the spring equinox. This is why it always falls on February 4th or 5th. We begin the five elements with wood, so the Chinese New Year begins with a wood month, whether in the Lunar or the Solar calendar. These concepts are derived from the Yi Jing.

## How to find your Animal Sign

To find your animal sign, start with your birth date. If it is before February 4th (Spring Begins), use the prior year for the Chinese calendar. If it is after February 4th, then use the same birth year. If it is on February 4th, then you need the time of the birth to accurately determine the birth animal. This information is contained in the Chinese Ten-Thousand Year Calendar. (The American Feng Shui institute has one available as an ebook at www.amfengshui.com). In the following pages, the birth years are listed for each animal, but remember, if your birthday is before February 4th, use the previous year to determine the animal.

## The Twelve Animals

| *Rat*  | *Ox*  | *Tiger*  | *Rabbit*  |
|---|---|---|---|
| 1924, 1936, 1948, 1960, 1972, 1984, 1996, 2008 | 1925, 1937, 1949, 1961, 1973, 1985, 1997, 2009 | 1926, 1938, 1950, 1962, 1974, 1986, 1998, 2010 | 1927, 1939, 1951, 1963, 1975, 1987, 1999, 2011 |
| *Dragon*  | *Snake*  | *Horse*  | *Sheep*  |
| 1928, 1940, 1952, 1964, 1976, 1988, 2000, 2012 | 1929, 1941, 1953, 1965, 1977, 1989, 2001 | 1930, 1942, 1954, 1966, 1978, 1990, 2002 | 1931, 1943, 1955, 1967, 1979, 1991, 2003 |
| *Monkey*  | *Rooster*  | *Dog*  | *Pig*  |
| 1932, 1944, 1956, 1968, 1980, 1992, 2004 | 1933, 1945, 1957, 1969, 1981, 1993, 2005 | 1934, 1946, 1958, 1970, 1982, 1994, 2006 | 1935, 1947, 1959, 1971, 1983, 1995, 2007 |

# FORTUNES OF THE 12 ANIMALS

# The Dragon

*Note: The New Year begins February 4th*

Year 2012 is the same animal as your birth year. This year contains sweet and bitter mixed together. Lots of unseen changes are in front of middle-aged Dragons. People born in 1976 will have good opportunities in sales, writing, and related to the finance industry. Your personality and impact on your surroundings will be in top form. You should be able to promote your ideas and plans successfully. Dragons born in 1964 who are bosses may encounter betrayal or misunderstanding by close partners. Beware of "petty men" backstabbers. Be patient and humble to avoid conflict. Money luck moves like a bouncing ball - up and down. Watch out for unexpected consuming so avoid being carried away by expensive plans and activities. Be particularly cautious in the months of April and October. In health, it will be easy to have some sort of bleeding; therefore avoid risky sports, climbing high, car accidents, and cuts. In romance, generally speaking, Dragons will be quite emotional, easily aroused to argue, and may lose control. Married or attached Dragons born in January, May, and August will find it easy to have a lot of quarrels this year, so take care and control your temper if you don't want your relationship to break up. Caution is the watchword of the year.

## Your Benefactor is: Ox
(1925, 1937, 1949, 1961, 1973, 1985, 1997, 2009)

# 12 Month Outlook For The Dragon

| Solar Month | Comments |
|---|---|
| **1st Month**<br>Feb 4th - Mar 4th | This is a relatively uneasy month: Do not be overconfident. Advice about risky investment is untrustworthy. |
| **2nd Month**<br>Mar 5th - Apr 3rd | An excellent time to tackle a new project. This is also a stimulating period intellectually. Take a class or start a new hobby. |
| **3rd Month**<br>Apr 4th - May 4th | Some obstacles lie ahead. Don't retain high expectations or be greedy about money matters beyond your capability. |
| **4th Month**<br>May 5th - Jun 4th | Sunny skies, life moves upward! |
| **5th Month**<br>Jun 5th - Jul 6th | Be conservative. Things are unstable and changing a lot this month. |
| **6th Month**<br>Jul 7th - Aug 6th | Not a beneficial time for going out late, at midnight. Be cautious of robbery. |
| **7th Month**<br>Aug 7th - Sep 6th | Auspicious luck. Things are to your satisfaction. |
| **8th Month**<br>Sep 7th - Oct 7th | Good opportunities come your way. Daily activities and surroundings are enjoyable. |
| **9th Month**<br>Oct 8th - Nov 6th | Keep on high alert. There is a sign of financial loss or bleeding. |
| **10th Month**<br>Nov 7th - Dec 6th | Things are uncertain. A wait and see attitude is the best policy. |
| **11th Month**<br>Dec 7th - Jan 4th | Backstabbers are around. You will be easily caught in squabbles. |
| **12th Month**<br>Jan 5th - Feb 3rd | Luck is noticeably moving upward. Unexpected benefits may be received on a long-distance vacation. |

# The Snake

*Note: The New Year begins February 4th*

With auspicious stars shinning above, this should be considered quite a smooth year for the Snakes. Expanding the business or getting a promotion is easy if the Snake proceeds in a bold, but with cautious manner. This is an exceptionally good year for venturing overseas to push on with the career for the self-employed. You will experience good fortune if you venture abroad whether it is for studies, career or emigration. There are signs of unexpected gains and benefactors. Though you will meet with a lot of competition and pressure in your work, luck is on your side. It is a year for making plans or learning something new. Students can expect good academic results. Salaried workers may discover a new source of income. In health, there are no signs of major problems; this year your common complains are headaches and allergies. In romance, generally speaking, female Snakes will be quite emotional, and may easily lose control. Yet, it is a good year for the Snakes born in the Spring and Autumn. Romance frequently signals good fortune, but if you abuse this energy and live a life of excess, it will cause trouble. You could be tempted to get involved in a secret love affair.

## Your Benefactor is: Rat
(1924, 1936, 1948, 1960, 1972, 1984, 1996, 2008)

# 12 Month Outlook For The Snake

| Solar Month | Comments |
|---|---|
| **1st Month**<br>Feb 4th - Mar 4th | Caution is the watchword of the month. What you are thinking may be the opposite of what it is. |
| **2nd Month**<br>Mar 5th - Apr 3rd | Stress will be higher than usual.<br>Tense relationships with friends or family. |
| **3rd Month**<br>Apr 4th - May 4th | Average luck. Things go smoothly and you will be happy due to strong peach blossom luck. Lots of social opportunities. |
| **4th Month**<br>May 5th - Jun 4th | Keep on high alert. Something sweet can become sour. |
| **5th Month**<br>Jun 5th - Jul 6th | Things are good for male but not for female Snakes. Conflicts and stress will be difficult for females to avoid. |
| **6th Month**<br>Jul 7th - Aug 6th | Sunny skies, life moves upward! Good time for a fresh start or new plans. |
| **7th Month**<br>Aug 7th - Sep 6th | It is a good month to focus on your target and work hard. The results will be as planned. Look out for minor cuts or burns. |
| **8th Month**<br>Sep 7th - Oct 7th | Good in love and career luck! Opportunity for promotion. |
| **9th Month**<br>Oct 8th - Nov 6th | Things are average to good, and busy. Money luck is sailing smoothly. |
| **10th Month**<br>Nov 7th - Dec 6th | Be cautious of something you were careless of before and avoid gambling or risky investment. |
| **11th Month**<br>Dec 7th - Jan 4th | Take care of your physical health. Watch out for some illness or the flu. |
| **12th Month**<br>Jan 5th - Feb 3rd | Luck is good. The plans and efforts you extend will be rewarded in future. |

# The Horse

*Note: The New Year begins February 4th*

Generally speaking, this is a mixed year for the Horse, alternating between auspicious and inauspicious. In career, you should put in more time and work hard; obstacles in the beginning can be overcome and will ultimately benefit you. When dealing with colleagues or friends, care must be taken to prevent acts of sabotage by others because of jealousy. In the year of 2012, frustration, in the form of gossip or rumor will plague you. Try to be humble at all times to avoid a nasty situation. The self-employed will have more opportunities for further development than salaried workers. Money prospects are average. Money comes and goes easily for those doing business: there are signs of hidden consuming. Be cautious to budget wisely and be extra careful when signing any contract to prevent financial losses. Health-wise, watch out for backache and pain or other problems of limbs which are likely to be prolonged. There is an omen that it may be necessary to put on mourning clothes for the elderly in the family. Avoid attending funerals. Where romance is concerned, it will be sensitive and complicated. An extraordinary relationship will show up in an unexpected way for singles. There is danger of married Horses getting into a scandalous affair. Horses born in 1954 and 1966 should watch out for signs of their lover's unfaithfulness.

## Your Benefactor is: Pig
### (1923, 1935, 1947, 1959, 1971, 1983, 1995, 2007)

# 12 Month Outlook For The Horse

| Solar Month | Comments |
|---|---|
| **1st Month**<br>Feb 4th - Mar 4th | Auspicious stars are shining above! Smooth sailing. |
| **2nd Month**<br>Mar 5th - Apr 3rd | Pay attention to your health to avoid minor illness. Avoid being overworked and take more time to relax. |
| **3rd Month**<br>Apr 4th - May 4th | A month of good and bad mixed. You will find conflicts and pressure on your job. |
| **4th Month**<br>May 5th - Jun 4th | Money prospects and career are in good sight. This is a great time to expand your career or develop something new. |
| **5th Month**<br>Jun 5th - Jul 6th | This is the month to be conservative and be on your guard for health. |
| **6th Month**<br>Jul 7th - Aug 6th | Things may look calm on the surface but there are hidden thorns within. |
| **7th Month**<br>Aug 7th - Sep 6th | Auspicious luck. Things are to your satisfaction. |
| **8th Month**<br>Sep 7th - Oct 7th | Be careful to avoid an illness which may come to you. To be safe, do not visit sick people or hospitals. |
| **9th Month**<br>Oct 8th - Nov 6th | Money luck is strong, a business venture will prove profitable. |
| **10th Month**<br>Nov 7th - Dec 6th | Good luck for social relationships and romance (Peach Blossom). A sunny time. |
| **11th Month**<br>Dec 7th - Jan 4th | Easy to be stabbed in the back. There will be some disharmony in a personal relationship. |
| **12th Month**<br>Jan 5th - Feb 3rd | Luck is noticeably moving upward. Work for your goal and it will come out quite well. |

# The Sheep

*Note: The New Year begins February 4th*

The Dragon year is one of mixed fortune for the Sheep. You should not set your expectations too high or you will spread yourself too thin. Resist new requests until you have fulfilled commitments already on your own schedule. Focus on what is most important first. Stick with it until you are satisfied with results. Only then should you move on to another task. Salaried worker will have more luck than the self-employed. Employers will be bogged down by problems such as a shortage of manpower, or you may find yourself betrayed by people working for you. The Sheep should avoid making investments on a whim in this Dragon year. Hold your emotions in check when you feel that you are becoming angered. Money prospects are good; the rewards will come from the effort you have put into your work, not as a result of a windfall. Be extra cautious in December as a wrong decision may result in financial losses. There are no signs of major health problems for the Sheep this year, but do take precautions against allergies and infectious diseases in the Spring and Summer. Where romance is concerned, the single Sheep will find this a relatively uneventful year, because certain things are beyond your control. Those born in 1967 and 1979 should watch out for signs of their lover's infidelity.

## Your Benefactor is: Rooster
### (1933, 1945, 1957, 1969, 1981, 1993, 2005)

# 12 Month Outlook For The Sheep

| Solar Month | Comments |
|---|---|
| **1st Month**<br>Feb 4th - Mar 4th | This is a relatively uneasy month: Do not be overly confident. Advice about risky investment is untrustworthy. |
| **2nd Month**<br>Mar 5th - Apr 3rd | Quite strong luck in career. Try to fight hard for what you want. |
| **3rd Month**<br>Apr 4th - May 4th | Some obstacles lie ahead. Your luck and mood are like a bouncing ball: high and low. |
| **4th Month**<br>May 5th - Jun 4th | Stay flexible throughout the month. Proceed slowly and deliberately with any changes you hope to enact. |
| **5th Month**<br>Jun 5th - Jul 6th | This month can bring conflict and tension. Walk away from an argument instead of being drawn into it. |
| **6th Month**<br>Jul 7th - Aug 6th | Good opportunities come your way. Daily activities and surroundings are easier than usual to handle. |
| **7th Month**<br>Aug 7th - Sep 6th | Things are not smooth and you may feel depressed. |
| **8th Month**<br>Sep 7th - Oct 7th | Backstabbers are around. You will easily be caught in squabbles. |
| **9th Month**<br>Oct 8th - Nov 6th | Things are uncertain. A wait and see attitude is the best policy. |
| **10th Month**<br>Nov 7th - Dec 6th | Lucky stars shine above! New opportunities come your way. |
| **11th Month**<br>Dec 7th - Jan 4th | Watch out for being cheated. Double-check all work, especially when done by others on your behalf. |
| **12th Month**<br>Jan 5th - Feb 3rd | Luck is noticeably moving upward. Compared to last month, things move fairly upward. |

# The Monkey

*Note: The New Year begins February 4th*

The Dragon year brings good tiding to the Monkey. Career and money luck are strong. There are lots of opportunities waiting for you – grab this auspicious luck and work hard, even when you face some obstacles. They can be overcome and will ultimately benefit you. The more you work, the more you gain. Though you may face some pressures and competition in work, luck is on your side. However, there is a sign of conflict in relationships. The Monkey's problem in 2012 is how to handle trouble with people and tangled up relationships. Maintain a low profile and stay humble when dealing with people. Don't make rude criticisms when you are feeling emotional. Otherwise, you will easily get stabbed in the back and this may slow down your efforts and luck. Career and money luck are at their best in the Spring and early Summer. In general, males receive stronger luck than females. Health-wise, this is quite an unstable year. Minor illness may easily visit you, and injury to your limbs may results from accidents. Those born in 1956 and 1968 should refrain from visiting the sick. Where romance is concerned, your love life is full of setbacks, so it will be quite a while before you find a true love. Though you may date quite a lot, it is difficult to differentiate a sincere relationship from one that is not. Married couples will blow hot and cold and quarrels will be easily aroused.

**Your Benefactor is:** Sheep
(1919, 1931, 1943, 1955, 1967, 1979, 1991)

# 12 Month Outlook For The Monkey

| Solar Month | Comments |
|---|---|
| **1st Month** Feb 4th - Mar 4th | This is a relatively uneasy month: Beneficial for venturing overseas. |
| **2nd Month** Mar 5th - Apr 3rd | Some luck is foreseen in money matters. Concentrate on work and business affairs. Teamwork is favored. |
| **3rd Month** Apr 4th - May 4th | Auspicious luck. Make a list of what you hope to accomplish, your plans and efforts will be rewarded in the future. |
| **4th Month** May 5th - Jun 4th | Sunny skies. Some problems that will not go away deserve attention now. You can resolve them. |
| **5th Month** Jun 5th - Jul 6th | Luck looks average. Be careful of being cheated. |
| **6th Month** Jul 7th - Aug 6th | Be conservative. Don't retain high expectations or get greedy about money matters beyond your capability. |
| **7th Month** Aug 7th - Sep 6th | Auspicious luck. Things are to your satisfaction. |
| **8th Month** Sep 7th - Oct 7th | There will be a number of squabbles. Be on your guard. You will meet someone fancy, but the relationship will turn sour. |
| **9th Month** Oct 8th - Nov 6th | Be careful of your health to avoid an illness which may visit you or one of the elderly family members. |
| **10th Month** Nov 7th - Dec 6th | Stress and tension could be higher than usual. |
| **11th Month** Dec 7th - Jan 4th | Luck is smooth for everything you plan. Most projects will hit the target. Career and money prospects are rewarding. |
| **12th Month** Jan 5th - Feb 3rd | Luck is noticeably moving upward. Life is enjoyable. |

# The Rooster

*Note: The New Year begins February 4th*

Year 2012 will bring wealth and fame for the Rooster. Career and money prospects are most promising. You may want to consider venturing abroad or pushing ahead with personal plans. Students can expect academic results. Seize this opportunity to take a big step forward and build your lifetime foundation. With extra strong luck, you will receive benefits in double for the work exerted. However, there is high pressure from competition for the self-employed. The Rooster can easily become stressed out and moody, so plenty of rest is recommended. Salaried workers will encounter a sign of conflicts with colleagues. There is a Chinese saying "Harmony breeds prosperity," so the best policy is to be humble at all times and try to maintain a cordial relationship with people around you. Health-wise, problems of digestive system, constipation and insomnia are common complaints this year. Romance is fruitful and sparkles! This is a good year for the single Rooster to get married but avoid ruining a perfect relationship in a moment of willfulness. This is also an easy year for the female Rooster to get pregnant. There is quite strong Peach Blossom for both the male and the female Rooster in this Dragon year, so the married Rooster should not try to pick that wild blossom from the roadside. Otherwise you will find it difficult to get rid of and will get quite a headache.

**Your Benefactor is:** Monkey
(1920, 1932, 1944, 1956, 1968, 1980, 1992, 2004)

# 12 Month Outlook For The Rooster

| Solar Month | Comments |
|---|---|
| **1st Month**<br>Feb 4th - Mar 4th | Luck goes smoothly for most everything. |
| **2nd Month**<br>Mar 5th - Apr 3rd | Backstabbers are around. You will be easily caught in squabbles. |
| **3rd Month**<br>Apr 4th - May 4th | Money luck is sailing smoothly, things are average to good. |
| **4th Month**<br>May 5th - Jun 4th | Good opportunities come your way. Daily activities and surroundings are enjoyable. |
| **5th Month**<br>Jun 5th - Jul 6th | Be conservative. Things are unstable and changing a lot this month. |
| **6th Month**<br>Jul 7th - Aug 6th | Luck will be bumpy. When you gain, watch out for possible loss. |
| **7th Month**<br>Aug 7th - Sep 6th | A spring wind blows over the land and feels so good. You are taking big steps forward in career |
| **8th Month**<br>Sep 7th - Oct 7th | Be patient and avoid becoming too emotional. Don't expect too much this month. |
| **9th Month**<br>Oct 8th - Nov 6th | Work toward your goal and it will come out quite well. |
| **10th Month**<br>Nov 7th - Dec 6th | Maintain high alert: no alcohol, no gambling, don't go out late to bars or entertainment places |
| **11th Month**<br>Dec 7th - Jan 4th | Partly sunny skies, lots of opportunities, lots of gossip around. |
| **12th Month**<br>Jan 5th - Feb 3rd | Luck is climbing up. The things you plan will be under control. There is a hidden gold opportunity! |

# The Dog

*Note: The New Year begins February 4ᵗʰ*

Because 2012 is the Po Sui or year breaker for the Dogs, generally you should not be overly optimistic this year. Things will change beyond your control. These changes, whether pre-planned or unexpected, will affect your career or business. No matter if you are salaried or self-employed, you may encounter one obstacle after another. Work will take double effort to receive a single measure of gain. Money luck is not what you expected; it is difficult to keep and save but it goes out easily. Be careful of over-spending and unexpected expenditures. Stay away from gambling. Moreover, there is a danger sign of getting entangled in legal problems. To avoid legal trouble, don't do anything risky. Pay attention to your health in late Autumn since it is easy to experience illness or injury, especially from sharp metal objects. Take measures to prevent colds; you may require a check-up for your lungs and chest. The path to romance is not going to be smooth; it is full of hiccoughs for singles. Do not expect too much from relationships. You will only be asking trouble if you ignore the unfavorable time factor and persist in being willful and overly passionate. Married Dog will be quite emotional and lose control. Be more communicative with your partner to avoid misunderstanding.

## Your Benefactor is: Tiger
### (1926, 1938, 1950, 1962, 1974, 1986, 1998, 2010)

# 12 Month Outlook For The Dog

| Solar Month | Comments |
|---|---|
| **1st Month**<br>Feb 4th - Mar 4th | Be conservative. Things are changing a lot this month. |
| **2nd Month**<br>Mar 5th - Apr 3rd | Compared to last month, things move fairly upward.  |
| **3rd Month**<br>Apr 4th - May 4th | A number of obstacles and setbacks may arise. Keep your emotions in check when dealing with people to avoid a bad outcome. |
| **4th Month**<br>May 5th - Jun 4th | This is a relatively unstable month: Do not be overly confident. Advice about risky investment is untrustworthy. |
| **5th Month**<br>Jun 5th - Jul 6th | Luck is noticeably moving upward, yet this is not the year for the Dog, so you still pay more and receive less. |
| **6th Month**<br>Jul 7th - Aug 6th | Not a beneficial time for going out late, at midnight. Be cautious of robbery. |
| **7th Month**<br>Aug 7th - Sep 6th | Things will be relative peaceful except for the third week of the month, when you should watch out for financial mishaps. |
| **8th Month**<br>Sep 7th - Oct 7th | Average luck, but prevent over spending for no reason.  |
| **9th Month**<br>Oct 8th - Nov 6th | Keep on high alert. There is a sign of financial loss or bleeding. |
| **10th Month**<br>Nov 7th - Dec 6th | Luck is smooth for everything you plan. Most projects will hit the target. Career and money prospects are rewarding.  |
| **11th Month**<br>Dec 7th - Jan 4th | Luck is unstable, good and bad are mixed. Hard work will provide high rewards. |
| **12th Month**<br>Jan 5th - Feb 3rd | Luck is steadily climbing up, all things come out well. It is a good time to think about something new. |

# The Pig

*1923, 1935, 1947, 1959, 1971, 1983, 1995, 2007*

*Note: The New Year begins February 4th*

Compared with last year, this is an auspicious year for the Pigs. Salaried workers can look forward to a promotion and raise while the self-employed are favorable for career developments. This is a highly rewarding year for the Pig! Numerous opportunities wait for Pigs in 2012. Yet this does not mean that you can sit at home and wait for the money to roll into your bank account; you must make full use of the year to work hard and fight for what you want. If you push ahead with your plans in the Spring and Summer, your career and money matters will end up satisfactorily. However, the self-employed must not use under-the-table ways to make money or you may lose everything. Even worse, you may get into trouble with law. Salaried workers will gain recognition in their workplace and there will be good prospects for promotion. There are signs of financial mishap taking place at your own home. Health-wise, there are no serious illnesses; you will be relatively healthy, but watch out for migraines and insomnia due to overwork. Where romance is concerned, it is not quite the same for singles and married couples. A fruitful relationship awaits singles this year. Autumn and Winter are the best times to build love nests. The love life of married couples will take a back seat because of not sharing the same feelings in daily matters; moreover, there are signs of certain things beyond your control, such as an unexpected intrusion of a third party.

## Your Benefactor is: Horse
### (1918, 1930, 1942, 1954, 1966, 1978, 1990, 2002)

# 12 Month Outlook For The Pig

| Solar Month | Comments |
|---|---|
| **1st Month**<br>Feb 4th - Mar 4th | Luck is up and down. This is a big consumer month. |
| **2nd Month**<br>Mar 5th - Apr 3rd | Auspicious stars gather inside the door. Big gains and small losses, good in all aspects. |
| **3rd Month**<br>Apr 4th - May 4th | Luck alternates between good and bad. There are some obstacles to overcome. |
| **4th Month**<br>May 5th - Jun 4th | Be conservative. There are signs of setback in money luck. |
| **5th Month**<br>Jun 5th - Jul 6th | Luck is strong, a business venture will prove profitable. |
| **6th Month**<br>Jul 7th - Aug 6th | The auspicious stars shine above! New opportunities come your way. A long distance vacation may bring unexpected benefit. |
| **7th Month**<br>Aug 7th - Sep 6th | Things are not as smooth in the last two months, and you may feel depressed. |
| **8th Month**<br>Sep 7th - Oct 7th | These are good months for singles to offer or receive a marriage proposal! In career, focus on your target and work hard; things will come out as you plan. Stress and tension could also be higher than usual. |
| **9th Month**<br>Oct 8th - Nov 6th | |
| **10th Month**<br>Nov 7th - Dec 6th | There is a hidden sign of misunderstanding and conflicts. Be cautious of your speech in public to avoid unnecessary contention. |
| **11th Month**<br>Dec 7th - Jan 4th | Everything is stable this month. |
| **12th Month**<br>Jan 5th - Feb 3rd | Good gains and strong joyful Peach-Blossom! A long distance vacation may bring unexpected benefit. |

# The Rat

*Note: The New Year begins February 4ᵗʰ*

This is a moderate year for Rats with neither signs of danger nor of major breakthrough. Where career is concerned, your rewards will be proportional to the efforts you put in. Therefore, harder you work, the more you gain. There is a sign of conflicts in relationships. Be wary of a trusted partner or friend turning against or betraying you. The problem for the Rat in 2012 is how to handle trouble with people and tangled up relationships. Keep a low profile and stay humble when dealing with people. Don't make rude criticism when you feel emotional. Otherwise, you will easily get stabbed in the back and it may slow down your efforts and luck. Career and money luck alternate between auspicious and inauspicious. Be wary of business swindles. If you intend to go into a partnership in this Dragon year, it is beneficial to approach males born in the Pig year or females born in the Rooster year. It is not beneficial for partnerships with people born in the Dog year. Overall, health is not foreseen as a problem area for the Rat during 2012. Avoid stress brought on by overwork. Watch out for illness caused by fatigue. The Spring may bring about skin allergies. Single Rats may give little thought to romance early in the year as other matters predominate. However, someone you have considered primarily a working partner or team associate may occupy more of your attention. Married couples will blow hot and cold and quarrels will be easily aroused.

**Your Benefactor is:** Dog
(1922, 1934, 1946, 1958, 1970, 1982, 1994, 2006)

# 12 Month Outlook For The Rat

| Solar Month | Comments |
| --- | --- |
| **1st Month**<br>Feb 4th - Mar 4th | There is a hint of anger or despair. Keep your emotions under tight control in all situations to avoid conflicts. |
| **2nd Month**<br>Mar 5th - Apr 3rd | Expenses for the month are uncertain. Your usual good judgment is at low tide. |
| **3rd Month**<br>Apr 4th - May 4th | Auspicious luck. Make a list of what you hope to accomplish, then begin it with item one and proceed downward. |
| **4th Month**<br>May 5th - Jun 4th | Relaxation is the top priority this month. Be cautious of illness. |
| **5th Month**<br>Jun 5th - Jul 6th | Double-check all work, especially when done by other people on your behalf. |
| **6th Month**<br>Jul 7th - Aug 6th | Lots of confusion in dealing with things.<br>Be cautious of scandals, and money losses. |
| **7th Month**<br>Aug 7th - Sep 6th | Auspicious luck. Things are to your satisfaction. |
| **8th Month**<br>Sep 7th - Oct 7th | Tense relationships with friends or family. |
| **9th Month**<br>Oct 8th - Nov 6th | This is a rewarding month! You can achieve your goals. |
| **10th Month**<br>Nov 7th - Dec 6th | Normal luck. Business ventures at a distance are promising. |
| **11th Month**<br>Dec 7th - Jan 4th | Average luck. You feel busy physically and mentally. |
| **12th Month**<br>Jan 5th - Feb 3rd | Enjoyable Peach Blossom. Partnerships of love are strengthened. Your mate or date knows just how to keep you smiling. |

# The Ox

*Note: The New Year begins February 4th*

The female Ox will find the Dragon a blessed year. Good news can be expected within the family. Career and money prospect are favorable. Everything will come easy for you. Salaried workers can look forward to a promotion and raise while the self-employed can expand their business. Yet, the male Ox's fortune alternates between good and bad this year. Be practical in whatever you do. You should act within the confines of your own abilities. Do not trust anyone blindly lest you get cheated. You will find it more rewarding to do everything on your own. Salaried workers should be careful of disputes with superiors or colleagues over trivial matters; mind your own business and walk away from an argument instead of being drawn into it. Health-wise, frequent bouts of moodiness and depression may lead to insomnia. Those born in 1973 should refrain from overworking lest they be stricken by illness. Try to relax as much as you can. Where romance is concerned, a fruitful relationship awaits the female this year. You will be able to walk down the aisle successfully and form a perfect union. Unfortunately, the male does not share the same luck. Romantic relationships are unstable and could be ruined by a third party. There are danger signs for married couples getting involved in scandalous affairs.

**Your Benefactor is:** Dragon
(1928, 1940, 1952, 1964, 1976, 1988, 2000, 2012)

# 12 Month Outlook For The Ox

| Solar Month | Comments |
|---|---|
| **1st Month**<br>Feb 4th - Mar 4th | Powerful sign of luck. Hard work will achieve favorable results. |
| **2nd Month**<br>Mar 5th - Apr 3rd | Nothing seems to go smoothly. It is easy to get involved in conflict with others. |
| **3rd Month**<br>Apr 4th - May 4th | Watch out for documentation errors. This is not a good time to sign contracts. |
| **4th Month**<br>May 5th - Jun 4th | It is a good time to focus on your target and work hard; the results will be what you planned. |
| **5th Month**<br>Jun 5th - Jul 6th | This month holds good fortune for proceeding with something new or expanding your career. |
| **6th Month**<br>Jul 7th - Aug 6th | Not a beneficial time for travelling or going out late, at midnight. Be cautious of robbery. |
| **7th Month**<br>Aug 7th - Sep 6th | Average luck. Watch out for the flu or cuts. |
| **8th Month**<br>Sep 7th - Oct 7th | Career and money prospects are good. |
| **9th Month**<br>Oct 8th - Nov 6th | Luck is low. To be safe, pay more attention to your health and do not visit sick people. |
| **10th Month**<br>Nov 7th - Dec 6th | Average luck. Relaxation is the top priority. |
| **11th Month**<br>Dec 7th - Jan 4th | There are signs of unexpected gains. Exceptionally good for venturing overseas. |
| **12th Month**<br>Jan 5th - Feb 3rd | Money prospects are at their best for females. Life is average for males. |

# The Tiger

*Note: The New Year begins February 4th*

This is a year to be conservative and not to be aggressive for self-employed Tigers. Be forewarned of some obstacles you will encounter. Career and money prospects alternate between good and bad. Overall, money luck this year indicates that unexpected consuming cannot be avoided. Beware of being cheated or sold out by others. Salaried workers should consider taking classes in self-improvement or job-related courses. It is a year of pressure for the Tigers. There is a general feeling of helplessness and frustration, especially in late Summer. Try not to get involved in matters that do not concern you to prevent trouble and loss. Investments should be made only after careful consideration. Learn to spend your money wisely and avoid financial speculation. July is the time to be on guard. Those born in 1962 should watch out for robbery or break-ins. Windfalls are not forthcoming in this year. Avoid financial speculation and gambling. Health-wise, watch out for problems with the digestive system. Tigers born in 1974 are quite accident-prone in the summer. To prevent accidents and injuries, stay away from strenuous sports and avoid scaling heights. It is going to be a complicated and confusing year for romance. To avoid being cheated, refrain from giving too much in a relationship. Married Tigers have a tendency to get involved in extramarital affairs.

## Your Benefactor is: Rabbit
(1927, 1939, 1951, 1963, 1975, 1987, 1999, 2011)

# 12 Month Outlook For The Tiger

| Solar Month | Comments |
|---|---|
| **1st Month**<br>Feb 4th - Mar 4th | Gossip will tangle things up. Things are not smooth. You may feel moody and impatient. |
| **2nd Month**<br>Mar 5th - Apr 3rd | Be conservative. Be alert for signs of money loss. |
| **3rd Month**<br>Apr 4th - May 4th | Your luck and mood are like a bouncing ball: high and low. |
| **4th Month**<br>May 5th - Jun 4th | Stay flexible throughout the month. Proceed slowly and deliberately with any changes you hope to enact |
| **5th Month**<br>Jun 5th - Jul 6th | Auspicious stars shine above! Good fortune goes hand in hand with you and puts you in the right place at the right time. |
| **6th Month**<br>Jul 7th - Aug 6th | This month can bring conflict and tension Take a back seat and relax. |
| **7th Month**<br>Aug 7th - Sep 6th | Luck is climbing up. If you plot future plans with care, the benefits will be everything you could hope for. |
| **8th Month**<br>Sep 7th - Oct 7th | Things are uncertain. Beware of Peach Blossom temptations (sex and alcohol). |
| **9th Month**<br>Oct 8th - Nov 6th | A long distance vacation may bring unexpected benefit. |
| **10th Month**<br>Nov 7th - Dec 6th | Strong Peach Blossom, yet results will not be favorable. |
| **11th Month**<br>Dec 7th - Jan 4th | Be cautious. Do not go too fast. Slow down and double-check what has been decided. |
| **12th Month**<br>Jan 5th - Feb 3rd | A rewarding month. All things come out well. |

# The Rabbit

*Note: The New Year begins February 4th*

2012 is a year of mixed good and bad for the Rabbit. Throughout, the Rabbits should take careful note of all that is going on around as well as keeping aware of the views of others. Numerous opportunities as well as obstacles await the Rabbit this year. Sudden changes may throw your life into disarray. Be conservative, this is not a good time to expand or switch careers. You need to be very careful if you plan to make investments. It is best to cut your losses by avoiding gambling and financial speculation altogether. However, it will be a good idea to travel abroad for work or study; there are good prospects for overseas ventures for working people and good academic results for those still in school. Again, care is needed; there is a sign of being cheated. With many temptations to spend, the year calls for careful financial management and restraint. It is not a time for taking risks. Health-wise, Due to the "Bing Fu" Star in Ming Palace, this is quite an unstable year. Minor illness may visit you non-stop. Those born in 1951 and 1963 should refrain from visiting the sick or attending wakes. Romance is not going to be plain sailing this year, so it is natural for you to feel empty and lonely. Disputes with your loved one will occur frequently. This is especially true for married Rabbits born in 1963.

**Your Benefactor is:** Snake
(1929, 1941, 1953, 1965, 1977, 1989, 2001)

# 12 Month Outlook For The Rabbit

| Solar Month | Comments |
|---|---|
| **1st Month** <br> Feb 4th - Mar 4th | Auspicious stars shine above! Fight hard for what you want and you will get it. |
| **2nd Month** <br> Mar 5th - Apr 3rd | Caution is the watchword of the month. What you are thinking may be the opposite of what is. |
| **3rd Month** <br> Apr 4th - May 4th | This month holds good fortune for money prospects. |
| **4th Month** <br> May 5th - Jun 4th | Things will go mostly as you wish. Whether working for a boss or for yourself, the results are secured when you apply extra effort now. |
| **5th Month** <br> Jun 5th - Jul 6th | Upsets may crop up when you least expect them. A project that has been moving under a full head of steam may sudden grind to a halt. |
| **6th Month** <br> Jul 7th - Aug 6th | Conditions are easy going and comfortable. |
| **7th Month** <br> Aug 7th - Sep 6th | There might be conflict with others. Be humble, as excessive self-esteem will lead to negative results. |
| **8th Month** <br> Sep 7th - Oct 7th | Things are average to good. Watch out for the flu. |
| **9th Month** <br> Oct 8th - Nov 6th | Be cautious of scandal. There is lots of confusion in dealing with things. |
| **10th Month** <br> Nov 7th - Dec 6th | Quite strong luck in career. Try to fight hard for what you want. |
| **11th Month** <br> Dec 7th - Jan 4th | Conflict arises easily. Be cautious in your speech and think before taking action. |
| **12th Month** <br> Jan 5th - Feb 3rd | Things are steadily moving up. Travel can put you in contact with someone who benefits your career in the future. |

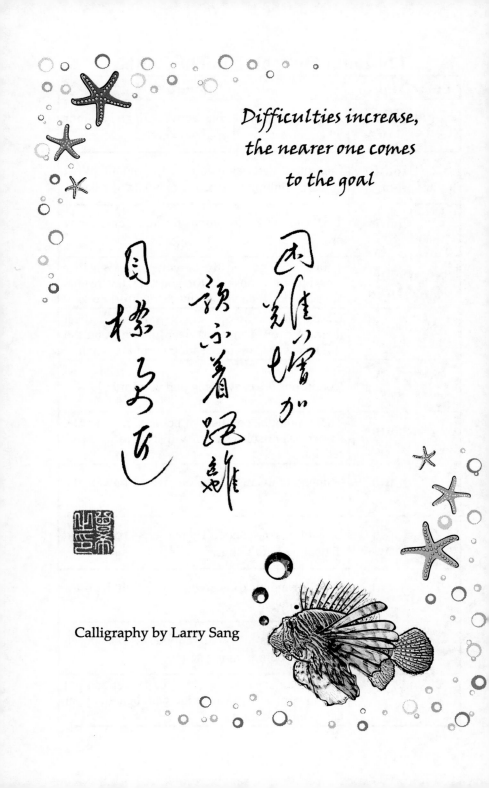

*Difficulties increase,*
*the nearer one comes*
*to the goal*

Calligraphy by Larry Sang

# LI MING

# TABLE 1

## 立 命 LI MING (establish fate): STEP 1: DETERMINE YOUR PALACE

## 立 命 LI MING for 2012

This is another system for making annual predictions:

★ First, use Table 1, based on your month and time of birth.

★ Take the results of Table 1, and use them in Table 2, along with your year of birth, to find the palace of Li Ming for 2012.

★ Once you know the palace of Li Ming, read the prediction that follows for that palace.

### Born After:

| Birth Hour: | | Jan 21 1st Month | Feb 19 2nd Month | Mar 20 3rd Month | Apr 20 4th Month | May 21 5th Month | Jun 21 6th Month | Jul 23 7th Month | Aug 23 8th Month | Sep 23 9th Month | Oct 23 10th Month | Nov 22 11th Month | Dec 22 12th Month |
|---|---|---|---|---|---|---|---|---|---|---|---|---|---|
| Zi | 11pm-1am | Mao | Yin | Chou | Zi | Hai | Xu | You | Shen | Wei | Wu | Si | Chen |
| Chou | 1-3am | Yin | Chou | Zi | Hai | Xu | You | Shen | Wei | Wu | Si | Chen | Mao |
| Yin | 3-5am | Chou | Zi | Hai | Xu | You | Shen | Wei | Wu | Si | Chen | Mao | Yin |
| Mao | 5-7am | Zi | Hai | Xu | You | Shen | Wei | Wu | Si | Chen | Mao | Yin | Chou |
| Chen | 7-9am | Hai | Xu | You | Shen | Wei | Wu | Si | Chen | Mao | Yin | Chou | Zi |
| Si | 9-11am | Xu | You | Shen | Wei | Wu | Si | Chen | Mao | Yin | Chou | Zi | Hai |
| Wu | 11am-1pm | You | Shen | Wei | Wu | Si | Chen | Mao | Yin | Chou | Zi | Hai | Xu |
| Wei | 1-3pm | Shen | Wei | Wu | Si | Chen | Mao | Yin | Chou | Zi | Hai | Xu | You |
| Shen | 3-5pm | Wei | Wu | Si | Chen | Mao | Yin | Chou | Zi | Hai | Xu | You | Shen |
| You | 5-7pm | Wu | Si | Chen | Mao | Yin | Chou | Zi | Hai | Xu | You | Shen | Wei |
| Xu | 7-9pm | Si | Chen | Mao | Yin | Chou | Zi | Hai | Xu | You | Shen | Wei | Wu |
| Hai | 9-11pm | Che | Mao | Yin | Chou | Zi | Hai | Xu | You | Shen | Wei | Wu | Si |

### Notes:

These months are different from the solar (Feng Shui/Four Pillars) months, and also are different from the lunar months. They begin on the *Qi* of the *Twenty-Four Jieqi*. If born within a day of these month dates, please consult a *Ten-Thousand Year Calendar* to determine exactly which is your birth month in this system. It is not necessary for you to understand the Chinese terms in the tables. Just follow the tables to the correct palace for you.

# TABLE 2 立 命 — LI MING (establish fate):
## STEP 2: PALACE FOR A CHEN (DRAGON) YEAR

LI MING for 2012

| Li Ming: | Rat Zi | Ox Chou | Tiger Yin | Rabbit Mao | Dragon Chen | Snake Si | Horse Wu | Sheep Wei | Monkey Shen | Rooster You | Dog Xu | Pig Hai |
|---|---|---|---|---|---|---|---|---|---|---|---|---|
| **Birth Year:** | | | | | | | | | | | | |
| Zi | Shen | You | Xu | Hai | Zi | Chou | Yin | Mao | Chen | Si | Wu | Wei |
| Chou | You | Xu | Hai | Zi | Chou | Yin | Mao | Chen | Si | Wu | Wei | Shen |
| Yin | Xu | Hai | Zi | Chou | Yin | Mao | Chen | Si | Wu | Wei | Shen | You |
| Mao | Hai | Zi | Chou | Yin | Mao | Chen | Si | Wu | Wei | Shen | You | Xu |
| Chen | Zi | Chou | Yin | Mao | Chen | Si | Wu | Wei | Shen | You | Xu | Hai |
| Si | Chou | Yin | Mao | Chen | Si | Wu | Wei | Shen | You | Xu | Hai | Zi |
| Wu | Yin | Mao | Chen | Si | Wu | Wei | Shen | You | Xu | Hai | Zi | Chou |
| Wei | Mao | Chen | Si | Wu | Wei | Shen | You | Xu | Hai | Zi | Chou | Yin |
| Shen | Chen | Si | Wu | Wei | Shen | You | Xu | Hai | Zi | Chou | Yin | Mao |
| You | Si | Wu | Wei | Shen | You | Xu | Hai | Zi | Chou | Yin | Mao | Chen |
| Xu | Wu | Wei | Shen | You | Xu | Hai | Zi | Chou | Yin | Mao | Chen | Si |
| Hai | Wei | Shen | You | Xu | Hai | Zi | Chou | Yin | Mao | Chen | Si | Wu |

Notes:

★ Take the Palace of Li Ming, found in Table 1, and compare it to the year of birth to find the palace for 2012, a Chen (Dragon) year.

★ Use January 21st as the beginning of the new year for finding the birth year. If the date falls within one day of January 21st, check in a *Ten-Thousand Year Calendar* to be sure. If the birth date is between January 1st and January 20th, consider the person as belonging to the previous year in this system.

★ The predictions described below go from January 20th, 2012 until January 19th, 2013.

**Zi**

It will be a moderate year with neither signs of danger nor major breakthroughs or change. Conflict with others will arise frequently. Be wary of a trusted partner or friend turning against or betraying you. Salaried-worker easily get promoted or demoted. Give full attention to whatever you are working on. Avoid gambling or financial speculation, for it will be a losing game. Avoid stress brought on by over-working. Watch out for illness caused by fatigue.

**Chou**

Because a number of inauspicious stars mix with an auspicious star, females will enjoy better money luck and their career will go smoothly. Males do not share the same fortune as females. Luck is inconsistent. Obstacles will stand in the way of career and money prospects. Be practical in whatever you do. Act within the confines of your own abilities. Make your expectations realistic or you will be disappointed. Refrain from over-working lest you be stricken by illness.

**Yin**

Be patient and do not get discouraged easily. It is not a year to expand or to be overly optimistic. Whatever is accomplished requires double effort to receive a single gain. Indulgence brings unexpected consumption of small things. Try not to get involved in matters that do not concern you at all to prevent trouble and loss. Investments should be made only after careful consideration. There are signs of a job change or moving residence.

**Mao**

This year is mixed, alternating between auspiciousness and inauspiciousness. Numerous opportunities as well as obstacles await you this year. Things will easily become tangled. Restrain yourself if you do not want to ruin your relationship. Though there are signs of conflict in relationships and pressure from competition, things can be accomplished by expending great effort and being prudent in all matters. Avoid attending funerals.

**Chen**

Because the Tai Sui is above you, danger lurks this year. Lots of unseen changes are in front. Career and money luck have auspiciousness and inauspiciousness mixed together. There is a great deal of pressure and competition at work. Beware of backstabbers. Be patient and humble to avoid conflict. Money luck is like a bouncing ball - up and down. Watch out for unexpected consuming. There are signs of bleeding. Try to avoid risky sports, climbing high, and car accidents.

**Si**

If Li Ming here, you will find this year a blessed one. Good news can be expected within the family. Career and money prospect are in your favor. If self-employed, this is a good year for venturing overseas to push on with your career. Salaried workers can look forward to a promotion, raise, or a new source of income. Yet, be alert for signs of overspending or backstabbers. Do not trust anyone blindly lest you get cheated.

**Wu**

A number of inauspicious stars mix with an auspicious star. If Li Ming is here, luck alternates between good and bad. Be practical in whatever you do. Frustration, in the form of gossip or rumors, will plague you. Try to be humble at all time to avoid a nasty situation. There are signs of unexpected gains and unnecessary expenditures. Be extra-cautious when signing any contracts to prevent financial losses. Funerals are highly likely, but avoid attending them, if possible.

**Wei**

A year of challenge and instability. Prospects are mixed between sweet and sour, and it is not wise to rush into a hasty commitment. Resist new requests until you have fulfilled the commitments already on your schedule. Have realistic expectations or you will be disappointed. There is a strong possibility of a job-related move or career change. When on an overseas business trip, elevate your alert level to avoid conflict with others.

**Shen**

This year, auspicious stars shine above: all four seasons bring peace and prosperity. Money luck is strong. Big profits come to the business person. Employees receive promotions. Golden opportunities await you overseas. Everything is what you wish for. Grab this auspicious luck and work hard. The more you work, the more you gain. But you are likely to have trouble from romance. Those who are married should avoid getting involved in extramarital affairs.

**You**

If Li Ming is here, both career and money prospects are most promising. With extra-strong luck, you will receive benefits in double measure for the work exerted. Though this is a relatively good year, care must be taken to prevent acts of sabotage by others arising from jealousy. Because of high pressure from competition, you can easily become stressed out and moody, so plenty of rest is recommended. Travel can put you in contact with someone who benefits your career in the future.

**Xu**

This year the Sui Po is in your Ming Palace, and the Tai Sui is opposite you. It will be a year of breakthroughs or changes. Conflict with others will arise easily. This is not a year to expand or be overly optimistic. Things suddenly change beyond your control. With an inauspicious Da Hao star, money luck is not what you expected; this is a sign of increase in unnecessary expenditures. Watch out for cash-flow problems and budget wisely. It is unfavorable for legal affairs.

**Hai**

This is an excellent year to embark on a new career or expand an existing business. Good fortune goes hand in hand with you, putting you in the right place at the right time. Work hard to accomplish your goals, and do all that you can to boost business prospects. Career and money matters will end up satisfactorily. It will be a beautiful year of romance for singles. Those who are married should avoid getting involved in extramarital affairs.

# LIU REN

# LIU REN (六壬)(小六壬)

1. Great Peace
2. Back & Forth
3. Hastening Happiness
4. Red Mouth
5. Small Auspiciousness
6. Empty & Lost

## Calculation:

When something out of the ordinary spontaneously happens,
you can determine the meaning of the omen with *Liu Ren*.
Here is the calculation:

1. Use the left hand. Start in position 1, Great Peace (大安 da an)
   and always move clockwise.
2. Count clockwise through the six positions for today's *lunar*
   month. The Great Peace position corresponds to the first lunar
   month. (Refer to *Ten-Thousand Year Calendar* page at the end
   of this *Guide*. Find today's date, then read the month number at
   the top of the column).
3. Count the position found in Step 2 as the first day of the lunar
   month. Count clockwise through the six positions to today,
   the current day of the lunar month. (Find today's date in the *Ten-
   Thousand Year Calendar* page, then read the day number on the
   side at the end of the row).

4. Count the position found in Step 3 as the first double hour. Count clockwise through the six positions to the current double hour.
5. Look up the interpretation of this palace on page 44 - 45.

## Hour Table

| Hour | During Standard Time | During Daylight Savings Time |
|------|---------------------|------------------------------|
| 1 | 11 pm - 1 am | midnight to 2 am |
| 2 | 1 - 3 am | 2 - 4 am |
| 3 | 3 - 5 am | 4 - 6 am |
| 4 | 5 - 7 am | 6 - 8 am |
| 5 | 7 - 9 am | 8 - 10 am |
| 6 | 9 - 11 am | 10 - noon |
| 7 | 11 am - 1 pm | noon to 2 pm |
| 8 | 1 - 3 pm | 2 - 4 pm |
| 9 | 3 - 5 pm | 4 - 6 pm |
| 10 | 5 - 7 pm | 6 - 8 pm |
| 11 | 7 - 9 pm | 8 - 10 pm |
| 12 | 9 - 11 pm | 10 - midnight |

**Note:** for 11 pm to midnight during standard time, use the next day's date. For example, if it is 11:15 pm on February 12th, then count it as February 13th.

**Example:** March 2nd, 2012, 12:45 pm

A. Start in Position One.
B. March 2nd is in the column that says 2nd month at the top.
   So we go to Position Two.
C. March 2nd is the 10th day of the 2nd month.
D. Start where we left off in Position Two and call that 1.
   Count clockwise to the 10th position from there: Position Five.
E. Start in Position Five and count for the hour.
F. Whether it is Daylight Savings Time or not, 12:45 pm is the 7th hour. Count 7 positions, with Position Five and call that 1, and end up in Position Five.

This is the outcome:

Position Five is **Small Auspiciousness**
Read the interpretation on the next page and apply it to the situation.

# Interpretation

## 1. Great Peace (大安 da an):

The person in question has not moved at this time. This position belongs to wood element and the east. Generally in planning matters, use 1, 5, and 7. This position belongs to the four limbs. Helpful people are found in the southwest. Avoid the east. Children, women and the six domestic animals are frightened.

In Great Peace, every activity prospers. Seek wealth in the southwest. Lost items are not far away. The house is secure and peaceful. The person you expect has not left yet. Illness is not serious. Military generals return home to the fields. Look for opportunities and push your luck.

## 2. Back and Forth (留連 liu lian):

The person you expect is not returning yet. This position belongs to water element and the north. Generally in planning matters, use 2, 8, and 10. This position belongs to the kidneys and stomach. Helpful people are found in the south. Avoid the north. Children wander the road as disembodied spirits.

With Back and Forth, activities are difficult to achieve. You have not adequately planned for your goals. Official activities are delayed. Those who have gone do not return from their journey yet. Lost items appear in the south. Hurry and ask for what you want and you will get results. But guard against gossip and disputes. Family members for the moment are so-so.

## 3. Hastening Happiness (速喜 su xi):

The expected person arrives shortly. This position belongs to fire element and the south. Generally in planning matters, use 3, 6, and 9. This position belongs to the heart and brain. Helpful people are found in the southwest. Avoid the south. Children, women, and animals are frightened.

With Hastening Happiness, happiness arrives. Seek wealth toward the south. Lost items are found between 11 am and 5 pm if you ask a passerby about it. Official activities have blessing and virtue. Sick people have no misfortune. Auspicious for the fields, house, and the six livestock. You receive news from someone far away.

## 4. Red Mouth ( 赤口 chi kou)

An inauspicious time for official activities. This position belongs to metal element and the west. Generally in planning matters, use 4, 7, and 10. This position belongs to the lungs and stomach. Helpful people are found in the east. Avoid the west. Children are bewildered young spirits.

Red Mouth governs quarrels and disputes. Be cautious about legal matters. Quickly go search for lost items. Travelers experience a fright. The six domestic animals give you trouble. The sick should go to the west. Furthermore, you must guard against being cursed. Fear catching epidemic diseases.

## 5. Small Auspiciousness (小吉 xiao ji)

The expected person comes in a happy time. This person belongs to wood element and all directions. Generally in planning matters, use 1, 5, and 7. This position belongs to the liver and intestines. Helpful people are found in the southwest. Avoid the east. Children, women and the six domestic animals are frightened.

Small Auspiciousness is most auspicious and prosperous. Your road is smooth. Spirits come announcing good news. Lost items are located in the southwest. Travelers promptly arrive. Relations with others are extremely strong. Everything is harmonious. A sick person should pray to heaven.

## 6. Empty and Lost ( 空亡 kong wang)

News you expect does not come at this time. This position belongs to earth element. Generally in planning matters, use 3, 6, and 9. This position belongs to the spleen and brain. Helpful people are found in the north. Watch out for the health of your children. Males feel pressure. The activities of females get no results.

Spirits are often unreasonable or perverse. Seeking wealth is without benefit. There is disaster for travelers. Lost items will not appear. Official activities bring punishment and damage. Sick people meet a dark ghost. To be secure and peaceful, get release from calamity by sacrifice and prayer.

**Example:** You arrive at the airport, but your friend who was supposed to pick you up is not there and does not answer his cell phone. You use Liu Ren to find out what is going on.

### Today's time and date: December 12<sup>th</sup>, 2012, 2:12 pm

A. Start in Position One.
B. December 12th is in the column that says 10th month at the top. So we go to Position Four.
  December 12th is the 29th day of the 10th month.
  Start where we left off in Position Four and call that 1.
C. Count clockwise to the 29th position from there: Position Two.
  Start in Position Two and count for the hour.
  It is 2:12 pm, the 8th hour.
D. Count 8 positions, with Position Two as the beginning, and end up in Position Three.

This is the outcome:

**Position Three is Hastening Happiness**

Read the text and apply it to the situation. Hastening Happiness begins with "The expected person arrives shortly." You wait calmly for ten minutes and your ride arrives. He tells you traffic delayed him and he forgot his cell phone.

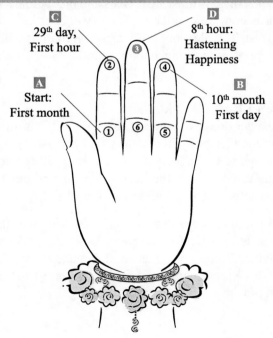

46

**OMEN**

# OMENS

In Chinese almanacs, there are often listings of predictions based on omens. We include a few below. Have fun with it and don't take it seriously.

## Omens from the Twitch of an Eye

| Time | Eye | This is an omen of: |
|---|---|---|
| 11 pm - 1 am Zi | Left | Meeting a benefactor |
| | Right | Having a good meal |
| 1 - 3 am Chou | Left | Having anxiety |
| | Right | Someone thinking about you |
| 3 - 5 am Yin | Left | Someone coming from afar |
| | Right | A happy matter arriving |
| 5 - 7 am Mao | Left | The coming of an important guest |
| | Right | Something peaceful, safe and auspicious |
| 7 - 9 am Chen | Left | A guest coming from afar |
| | Right | Injury or harm |
| 9 - 11 am Si | Left | Having a good meal |
| | Right | Something inauspicious |
| 11 am - 1 pm Wu | Left | Having a good meal |
| | Right | An inauspicious matter |
| 1 - 3 pm Wei | Left | A lucky star |
| | Right | Good luck, but small |
| 3 - 5 pm Shen | Left | Money coming |
| | Right | Someone thinking of you romantically |
| 5 - 7 pm You | Left | A guest coming |
| | Right | A guest arriving |
| 7 - 9 pm Xu | Left | A guest arriving |
| | Right | A gathering or meeting |
| 9 - 11 pm Hai | Left | A guest arriving |
| | Right | Gossip |

Correct for *Daylight Savings Time*, if in use (subtract one hour from the current time).

# Omens from Hiccoughs

| Time | This is an omen of: |
|---|---|
| 11 pm - 1 am<br>Zi | A good meal and a happy dinner gathering |
| 1 - 3 am<br>Chou | Someone missing you; a guest coming to seek your help |
| 3 - 5 am<br>Yin | Someone missing you; a dining engagement |
| 5 - 7 am<br>Mao | Wealth and happiness; someone coming to ask about a matter |
| 7 - 9 am<br>Chen | A good meal; great good luck for everyone |
| 9 - 11 am<br>Si | A lucky person coming to seek wealth |
| 11 am - 1 pm<br>Wu | An important guest; someone wanting a dinner gathering |
| 1 - 3 pm<br>Wei | Someone wanting a meal; lucky activities |
| 3 - 5 pm<br>Shen | Nightmares; eating is not beneficial |
| 5 - 7 pm<br>You | Someone coming; someone asks about a matter |
| 7 - 9 pm<br>Xu | Someone missing you; a meeting brings benefit |
| 9 - 11 pm<br>Hai | Something frightens, but on the contrary, brings benefit |

Correct for *Daylight Savings Time*, if in use (subtract one hour from the current time).

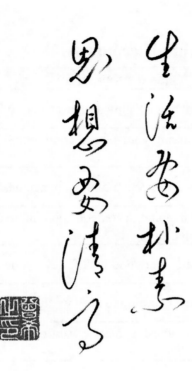

生活要樸素

思想要清高

Simple living
and
high thinking

Calligraphy by Larry Sang

# THE YELLOW EMPEROR

# THE YELLOW EMPEROR
# IN THE FOUR SEASONS

黃帝四季詩

SPRING — Zi, Mao, You, Chou, Hai, Si, Wei, Wu, Chen, Xu, Shen, Yin

AUTUMN — Hai, Zi, Wu, Mao, Wei, Si, Chou, Shen, Yin, You, Xu, Chen

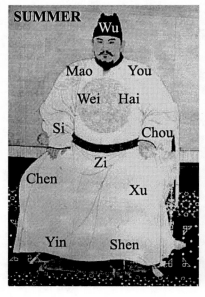

SUMMER — Wu, Mao, You, Wei, Hai, Si, Chou, Zi, Chen, Xu, Yin, Shen

WINTER — Si, You, Mao, Yin, Shen, Hai, Wu, Zi, Chou, Wei, Chen, Xu

There is a lifetime prediction commonly found in Chinese almanacs. Based on your season of birth, find your birth time.

## The Yellow Emperor in the Four Seasons

| Time of Birth | | Season of Birth | | | |
|---|---|---|---|---|---|
| | | Spring February 4th to May 4th | Spring February 4th to May 4th | Spring February 4th to May 4th | Spring February 4th to May 4th |
| Zi | 11p-1a | head | low abdomen | shoulders | low abdomen |
| Chou | 1-3a | chest | hands | hands | knees |
| Yin | 3-5a | feet | feet | knees | chest |
| Mao | 5-7a | shoulders | shoulders | chest | shoulders |
| Chen | 7-9a | knees | knees | feet | feet |
| Si | 9-11a | hands | hands | hands | head |
| Wu | 11a-1p | low abdomen | head | shoulders | hands |
| Wei | 1-3p | hands | chest | chest | knees |
| Shen | 3-5p | feet | feet | low abdomen | chest |
| You | 5-7p | shoulders | shoulders | knees | shoulders |
| Xu | 7-9p | knees | knees | feet | feet |
| Hai | 9-11p | chest | chest | head | hands |

Correct birth time for Daylight Saving Time, if used at the time of birth. If you were born in the Southern Hemisphere, switch the autumn and spring dates, as well as the summer and winter dates.

## The Yellow Emperor in the Four Seasons

**Born on the Yellow Emperor's Head** means a lifetime of never having worries. Even petty people have riches and honor. Clothes and food naturally come around. Your position in society is elevated, and gentlemen are good at planning. Women go through life steadily and smoothly, marrying a talented and educated person.

**Born on the Yellow Emperor's Hands** means business capital is sufficient. Going out, you meet a benefactor. Inside the home, you have everything. Your early years are very steady and smooth. You accumulate many possessions. Wealth comes from every direction. When old, it is in your hands.

## The Yellow Emperor in the Four Seasons

**Born on the Yellow Emperor's Shoulders** means a life of a million riches. You have wealth in your middle years. Children and grandchildren are plenty. Clothes and income at all times are good. In old age, you have fields in the village. Siblings are helpful. Your early life is bitter, but the later end is sweet.

**Born on the Yellow Emperor's Chest** means clothes and food are naturally ample. Experts in the pen and the sword are around you. There is music, song, and dance. Middle age brings good clothes and food. Later years are happy and prosperous. Joy, utmost honor, prosperity, and increased longevity add more blessings.

**Born on the Yellow Emperor's Lower Abdomen,** you were treasured by your parents. In middle age, clothes and food are good. When old you obtain gold. The family reputation is changing a lot. You are a noble person. Children and grandchildren must newly shine. Cultured and bright, they advance a lot.

**Born on the Yellow Emperor's Knees** means doing things is without benefit. In your early years, you toiled a lot, but did not lack clothes and food. Everyday, you travel on the road; you cannot avoid running back and forth. Old age is smooth, with honor and prosperity, but in middle age, hard work is extreme.

**Born on the Yellow Emperor's Feet,** practice moral teachings to avoid toil. A lifetime that is safe and sound, but unsuitable to reside in your ancestor's home. Women marry two husbands. Men have two wives. Search lonely mountain ranges. Leave your homeland to achieve good fortune.

# FENG SHUI

# FENG SHUI
## *Makes the Universe Work for You*

 We live in a universe that is filled with different energies. Our planet rotates on its axis, creating cycles of day and night. The earth also revolves around the sun in yearly cycles and is subject to various gravitational and magnetic fields. Our solar system is moving through space and is also subject to other forces in the universe. These physical forces and many different time cycles affects us profoundly. The Chinese have spent centuries observing the effects with their environment. This is the science and art of Feng Shui (Chinese geomancy).

Feng Shui uses observation, repeatable calculations and methodologies, and is based on the study of the environment, both inside and out of the house. Feng Shui can help you determine the best home to live in, which colors can enhance your home, the best bed positions for deep sleep, and how to change your business or home into a center of power. Feng Shui can help improve your health, your relationships and your prosperity. It is based on a complex calculation and observation of the environment, rather than a metaphysical reading relying on inspiration or intuition.

The American Feng Shui Institute publishes the annual Chinese Astrology and Feng Shui Guide so that both the Feng Shui professional and layperson can benefit from the knowledge of the incoming energy cycles and their influences. With this knowledge, one can adjust their environment to make it as harmonious as possible for the current year.

The following sections contain the energy patterns for the current year with an analysis and remedy for each of the eight directions. For the nonprofessional, there is a section on how to prepare your home for this reading. Please note that Feng Shui is a deep and complex science that requires many years to master. Preparing your home to receive the annual energy is one aspect that anyone can apply. A professional reading is recommended to anyone who wishes to receive the greatest benefits possible that Feng Shui can bring.

# Preparing your home for a Feng Shui reading

## The Floor Plan

The first requirement for preparing your home for a Feng Shui annual reading is to create a proportional floor plan. This plan can be hand drawn or be the original building plans, as long as the plan is proportionally correct. It is not necessary to draw in all your furniture except perhaps noting your bed and desk. It is important that you indicate where all window and door openings are.

**Example B Floor Plan**

**Example A Floor Plan**

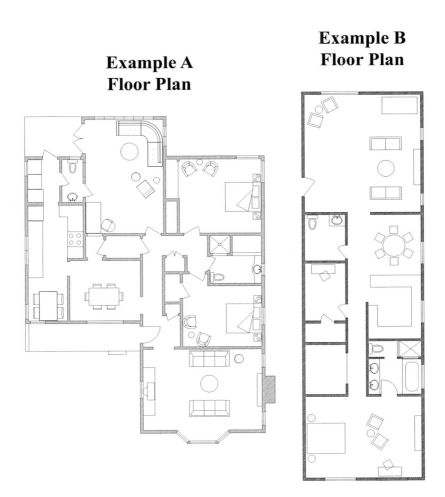

### Gridding The Floor Plan

Once you have your floor plan drawn, you then overlay a 9 - square grid. This grid is proportional to the floor plan. If it were a long and narrow house, so would the grid be long and narrow. You want to divide the floor plan into equal thirds both top to bottom and left to right as shown below:

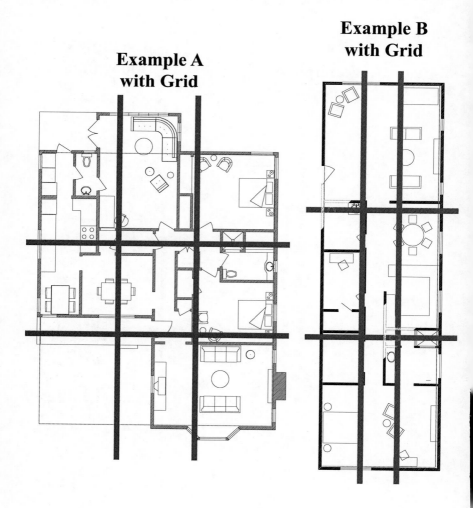

**Example B with Grid**

**Example A with Grid**

# The Compass Reading

The next step is to determine the alignment of your house with the earth magnetic fields by taking a compass reading. It is very important to take an accurate reading and not guess the orientation based on the direction of the sun or a map.

## Why Do You Need To Use A Compass?

In Feng Shui, we look at the eight cardinal and inter-cardinal directions: East, Southeast, South, Southwest, West, Northwest, North, and Northeast when analyzing a home or building. Each of these directions hold unique significance to these building. If you do not use a compass to determine the correct orientation, you might completely misread your home. You cannot map the qi within the building without an exact orientation. It is similar to finding your way out of a forest without a compass. You have a high probability of getting lost. Without a compass, it simply is not Feng Shui.

## A Compass vs A Luopan

You can use any compass if you do not have a Luopan. The Luopan is simply a Chinese compass that helps determine the sitting direction of a building. It also contains a wealth of information on its dial that is used for more advanced applications. In recent years, Master Larry Sang simplified the traditional Luopan specifically for training Western students. Although it looks simple compared to an original Luopan, it has all the tools you need to accurately analyze a building. An important fact to remember about a Luopan is that it points to the South. The following information and instructions apply to a Luopan, however, if you are using a Western compass these concepts are easy to adapt.

# SANG'S LUOPAN

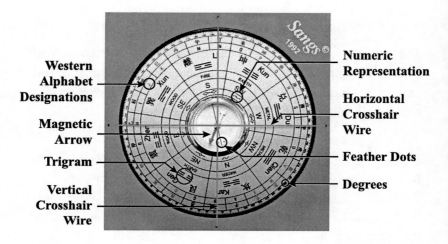

Western Alphabet Designations

Magnetic Arrow

Trigram

Vertical Crosshair Wire

Numeric Representation

Horizontal Crosshair Wire

Feather Dots

Degrees

## Parts of Sang's Luopan

**The Magnetic Arrow** - The arrowhead points South rather than North. Western compasses point North.

**The Feather Dots** - (The twin dots at the center of the rotating dial). Always adjust the rotating (gold) dial to align the twin dots with the feather end of the arrow.

**The Numeric Representations** - The innermost ring has a dot pattern that represents the Trigram' numbers. For example Kun has two dots and Qian has six dots.

**Crosshair Alignments** - The red crosshairs designate the facing and sitting directions. Once the arrow is steady and the feather end is aligned over the north twin dots, you can determine the sitting direction and the facing direction.

**The Eight Trigrams** - The Eight Trigrams are the basis for orientation in Feng Shui and are shown on the Luopan with their perspective elements, symbols, and directions.

**Western Alphabet Designations -** Each Trigram is divided into three equal parts. These parts are shown with both their Chinese symbols and using the Western Alphabet.

**The Degrees -** Outermost on the dial are the Western compass degree in Arabic numerals.

## General Guidelines for using the Luopan:

**To use the Luopan or compass correctly, remember the following guidelines:**

1. Always stand straight and upright.
2. Do not wear metal jewelry or belt buckles that can skew the compass.
3. Avoid any electrical influences such as automobiles or electrical boxes.
4. Always stand parallel to the building.
5. Keep your feet square below you.
6. You can keep the Luopan in the lower box case to manage it better.

## Taking a reading with the Luopan:

With the general guidelines for using a luopan in mind, now you ar ready to take a reading to determine which wall or corner of your home is located closest to the North.

1. Take your reading outside, standing parallel to your home with your back to it. Stand straight and hold the Luopan at waist level. Wait until the arrow ceases to quiver.

2. Slowly turn the center (gold) dial so that the North/feather dots aligh with the feather of the arrow. If using a Western compass, turn the compass so that the needle's arrow end aligns with north (between 337.5° - 22.5°).

3. Please take at least three separate readings from other positions. If you find that there is a discrepancy, take various readings at various locations until you are sure which one is correct. One direction should stand out as being correct.

4. Indicate on your floor plan which section is North. Fill in the other directions as illustrated. Please note that North can lie in a corner section.

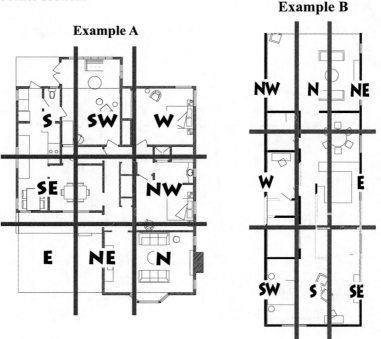

Example A

Example B

# DIRECTIONS TO AVOID FOR CONSTRUCTION 2012

## *The Three Sha and The Sui Po*

The **Three Sha** are in the **South (Southeast and Southwest)**: **Si, Wu** and **Wei** directions

The **Sui Po** or **Year Breaker** is in the **Northwest: Xu** direction. The **Tai Sui** is in the **Southeast: Chen** direction.

> Therefore, avoid using these directions:
> **Chen, Si, Wu, Wei** and **Xu**

### Directions to Avoid

| 15° Direction | Degrees | 45° Direction | Sang's Luopan Alpha Designation |
|---|---|---|---|
| Si | | SE | k |
| Bing | | | l |
| Wu | 142.5° - 217.5° | S | m |
| Ding | | | n |
| Wei | | SW | o |
| Chen | 112.5° - 127.5° | SE | i |
| Xu | 292.5° - 307.5° | NW | u |

### What should we avoid in these directions?

- New construction sitting in these directions (except Chen Southeast).
- Major renovation to buildings sitting in these directions (except Chen Southeast).
- Major renovation to this section of the house, regardless of the sitting direction.
- Burial of the deceased in these directions.
- Digging or breaking of earth in these directions. If digging cannot be avoided in any of these areas, then place a metal wind chime outside between the house and the digging site.
- In addition, Dragons or Dogs in the third, sixth, ninth or twelve month of the Chinese calendar should avoid attending funerals or burials.

# FENG SHUI

## 2012

**Qi Pattern**

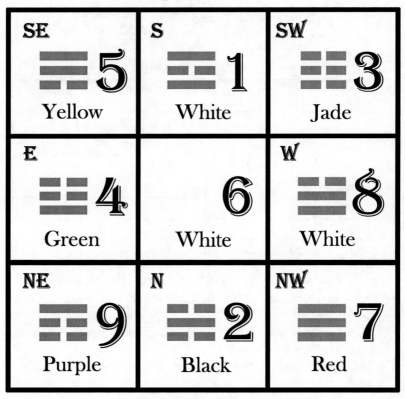

| | | |
|---|---|---|
| **SE** 5 Yellow | **S** 1 White | **SW** 3 Jade |
| **E** 4 Green | 6 White | **W** 8 White |
| **NE** 9 Purple | **N** 2 Black | **NW** 7 Red |

The Qi (energy) shift begins on
**February 4th at 6:40pm**

# INTRODUCTION

While this diagram may look foreign to the beginner, it is essential information for the experienced Feng Shui practitioner. Each year the qi pattern brings different effects. Some of these effects are quite auspicious and favorable and some may be inauspicious and not so favorable.

The effects of the 2012 energy pattern are analyzed for you in the following pages. Each analysis contains suggested remedies or enhancements for each section. Remedies are recommended to reduce negative qi. Enhancements are recommended to increase beneficial qi. These remedies or enhancements consist of the five elements: wood, fire, earth, metal, and water.

To use a remedy or enhancement, it must be placed inside the house within that particular section. If more than one room exists within a section, then each room needs to have its own remedy or enhancement. Any exceptions will be noted.

Feng Shui

# FENG SHUI  2012

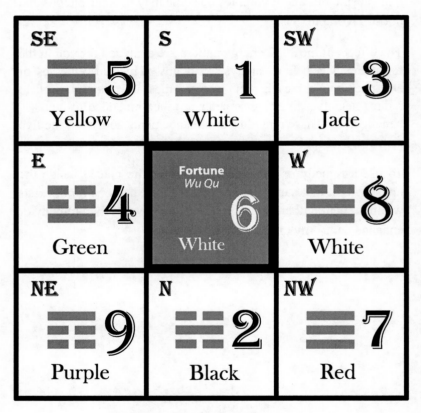

| SE | S | SW |
|---|---|---|
| **5** Yellow | **1** White | **3** Jade |
| E | **Fortune** *Wu Qu* | W |
| **4** Green | **6** White | **8** White |
| NE | N | NW |
| **9** Purple | **2** Black | **7** Red |

**The Center Section**

# Center

## Analysis

Last year (2011), the *7 Po Jun Star* visited the center. We are currently in period 8. The 8 White Star belongs to earth element which strengthened the Po Jun Star's (metal element) qi. The 7 Po Jun Star is competitive and fighting so we predicted the world would enter another era of "growth of fighting and conflict." Economic recovery might be slow and painful. This is all due to the Po Jun Star (metal element) reducing the earth qi of the center 8 White Wealth Star.

This year the *6 Fortunate Wu Qu Star* (powerful yang metal) is in the center, so it will be more unfavorable than last year. The Wu Qu star also is metal element; therefore we can predict that 2012 will not be a peaceful year. The worldwide economic crisis still lies ahead and we will see the start of currency and trade wars. Meanwhile, people may experience fighting, fire-related disasters such as forest fires, corruption exposed in political circles, and people protesting all over around the world. Real estate in the US will continue to fall. Chinese property prices will drop overall 20 to 35%.

Feng Shui

# FENG SHUI  2012

| | | |
|---|---|---|
| **SE** ☴ **5** Yellow | **S** ☲ **1** White | **SW** ☷ **3** Jade |
| **E** Literary *Wen Qu* ☳ **4** Green | **6** White | **W** ☱ **8** White |
| **NE** ☶ **9** Purple | **N** ☵ **2** Black | **NW** ☰ **7** Red |

**The East Section**

# East

## Situation

Doors, bedrooms, study rooms in the east section.

## Analysis

The *4 Green Wen Qu Literary Star* is in the east in 2012. The Literary Star represents creative and academic achievements and Peach Blossom. Its element is wood. The east section is the home of the 3 Jade Lu Cun Star, which is also wood element. Wood with wood creates a strong relationship. Moreover, there is one important auspicious yearly star entering this section. Therefore, making use of the east section will be beneficial for business expansion and bring strong romantic (peach blossom) qi. This is beneficial for literature, scholars, writers, artists, sales, students and people in the entertainment industry.

## Enhancement: Fire

A possible application of fire element can be a red light bulb, a lamp with a red shade or any red decorative item. The corresponding colors of maroon, purple or fuchsia can also be used.

## Caution

Strong Peach Blossom.
It is easy to encounter extramarital affairs.

# FENG SHUI  2012

| | | |
|---|---|---|
| **SE**<br>**Disaster**<br>*Lian Zhen*<br>**5**<br>Yellow | **S**<br>**1**<br>White | **SW**<br>**3**<br>Jade |
| **E**<br>**4**<br>Green | **6**<br>White | **W**<br>**8**<br>White |
| **NE**<br>**9**<br>Purple | **N**<br>**2**<br>Black | **NW**<br>**7**<br>Red |

## The Southeast Section

# Southeast

## Situation

Doors, bedrooms, study rooms in the southeast section.

## Analysis

The **5 Yellow Lian Zhen Disaster** Star visits the southeast this year. This star is also called the 5 Yellow Sha and Evil Influence Star or Yellow Pestilence Star. It brings the potential for delays, obstacles, fire, lawsuits, sickness, and casualty. The 5 Yellow Star is earth element. Southeast is the home location of 4 Green Wen Qu, a wood element star. Wood and metal have a relationship of domination. Therefore, if your bedroom falls in this section, the potential to develop tumors can exist if no remedy is applied. However, it is advisable to avoid spending a lot of time in this area. It is also critical to avoid ground breaking or construction in this direction, since it is easy to arouse misfortune.

## Remedy: Metal

To reduce the potential negative effects mentioned above, use a metal remedy in this area or direction. This can be a decorative metal sculpture or ornament. One with moving metal parts is preferable, such as grandfather clock.

## Caution

Don't do construction or digging in this direction.

# FENG SHUI

## 2012

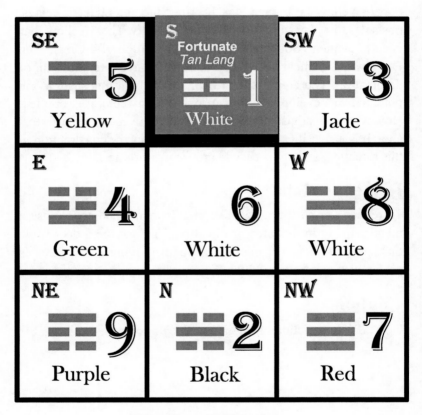

| | | |
|---|---|---|
| **SE** 5 Yellow | **S** Fortunate *Tan Lang* 1 White | **SW** 3 Jade |
| **E** 4 Green | 6 White | **W** 8 White |
| **NE** 9 Purple | **N** 2 Black | **NW** 7 Red |

**The South Section**

# South

## Situation

Doors, bedrooms, study rooms in the south section.

## Analysis

The *1 White Tan Lang Fortunate Star* is in the south this year. This Fortunate Star represents wealth, fame, romance and good negotiations. The element of the 1 White Star is water. The south is home to the 9 Purple Star which brings promotions and celebration. Though the individual nature of the 1 White Tan Lang Fortunate Star and the 9 Purple Star are auspicious, the south is the home base of fire element. Water and fire create an unharmonious domination relationship. The inauspicious Three Sha are also in the south, so avoid construction and digging in the south during this Dragon year. Otherwise, some unhappy things, such as bleeding, gun shots, or fire-related disaster can easily become aroused.

## Caution

Don't do construction or digging in this direction.
Not beneficial for jewelry, goldsmiths, or metal-related businesses.

## Remedy: Plants

Use indoor plants to remedy the unharmonious relationship.

## After Remedy

Beneficial for people in love to move toward the wedding chapel.

# FENG SHUI  2012

| SE | S | SW |
|---|---|---|
| ☶ **5** Yellow | ☷ **1** White | **Gossip** *Lu Cun* ☶ **3** Jade |
| **E** ☷ **4** Green | **6** White | **W** ☰ **8** White |
| **NE** ☷ **9** Purple | **N** ☵ **2** Black | **NW** ☱ **7** Red |

## The Southwest Section

# Southwest

## Situation

Doors, bedrooms, study rooms in the southwest section.

## Analysis

In 2012 the *3 Jade Green Lu Cun Star* visits the southwest. The 3 Jade Green Lu Cun Star is wood element. It is a star of fighting, robberies, arguments, misunderstandings and gossip. The southwest section is the home of the 2 black Ju Men Star, and its element is earth. Wood and earth have a relationship of domination, which creates disharmony in the family, especially for a housewife. Therefore, if spending a lot of time in the southwest, you should be cautious of health problems or sexually transmitted diseases. Moreover, this year has an inauspicious star, Sui Sha, in the Southwest, so it is not advisable to do any construction or ground breaking here, as misfortune from sickness or robbery is easily aroused.

## Caution

Don't do construction or digging in this direction.
Not beneficial for a housewife or elderly women to have this section as the bedroom.

## Remedy: Fire

Use a fire element remedy in this area. A possible application of fire element can be a red light bulb, a lamp with a red shade or any red decorative item. The corresponding colors of maroon, purple or fuchsia can also be used.

# FENG SHUI 2012

| | | |
|---|---|---|
| **SE** ䷗ **5** <br> Yellow | **S** ䷁ **1** <br> White | **SW** ䷁ **3** <br> Jade |
| **E** ䷁ **4** <br> Green | **6** <br> White | **W** **Money Star** *Zuo Fu* ䷁ **8** <br> White |
| **NE** ䷁ **9** <br> Purple | **N** ䷁ **2** <br> Black | **NW** ䷀ **7** <br> Red |

**The West Section**

# West

## Situation

Doors, bedrooms, study rooms in the west section.

## Analysis

This year the **8 White Zou Fu Wealth Star** arrives in the west. The 8 White Star belongs to earth element and is at its strongest during the current Period 8. The West is the home of the 7 Red Po Jun Star, which is metal element. These two stars, earth and metal, have a productive relationship and make this section one of the most auspicious areas in 2012. It can produce good money luck, fame, and some kind of new development or breakthrough. Making use of this area will be beneficial for new development, breakthroughs, wealth, and promotions.

## Benefits

Beneficial for new development, expansion, and breakthroughs. Prosperous for land developers, real estate, jewelry, goldsmiths, metal-related businesses.

## Enhancement: Earth

Use earth element, such as a decorative piece of glazed pottery or porcelain.

# FENG SHUI  2012

| | | |
|---|---|---|
| **SE** 5 Yellow | **S** 1 White | **SW** 3 Jade |
| **E** 4 Green | 6 White | **W** 8 White |
| **NE** 9 Purple | **N** 2 Black | **NW** Fighting *Po Jun* 7 Red |

## The Northwest Section

# Northwest

## Situation

Doors, bedrooms, study rooms in the northwest section.

## Analysis

This year the *7 Red Po Jun Fighting Star* is in the northwest. The 7 Po Jun Star is a competitive and fighting star. Its element is metal. Northwest is the home of the 6 White Fortune Star which is also metal element. Metal and metal create conflicts in relationships easily. Moreover, the inauspicious Po Sui Star is in the northwest. If the main entrance or bedroom falls in this section, be careful of conflicts with others, mostly due to challenge to the power of authority. Also be on guard for unexpected casualties such as gunshots, bleeding, or financial loss.

## Caution

Be on guard for unexpected casualties such as gunshots, bleeding, or financial loss.

## Remedy: Water

Use water element, such as a water fountain, aquarium, or the colors of blue or black.

Feng Shui

# FENG SHUI  2012

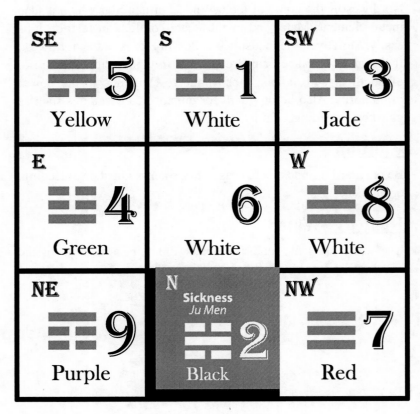

| | | |
|---|---|---|
| **SE**  5  Yellow | **S**  1  White | **SW**  3  Jade |
| **E**  4  Green | 6  White | **W**  8  White |
| **NE**  9  Purple | **N** Sickness *Ju Men*  2  Black | **NW**  7  Red |

**The North Section**

# North

## Situation

Doors, bedrooms, study rooms in the north section.

## Analysis

The *2 Black Ju Men Star* is in the north this year. The 2 Black Ju Men Star belongs to earth element and represents sickness, gossip, and misunderstandings. The north is the home of the 1 White Fortune Star, and it belongs to water element. The 2 Black Ju Men Star (earth element) and the 1 White (water element) have a relationship of domination. The north is also opposite the Three Sha inauspicious stars. Therefore, if spending a lot of time in this area, you should be cautious of health problems, sexually-transmitted diseases, and unfavorable legal affairs.

## Caution

Not beneficial for a pregnant or elderly women to stay in this area.

## Remedy: Metal

To reduce the potential negative effects mentioned above, use metal element as a remedy in this area. A metal remedy can consist of decorative metal décor, such as a piece of sculpture or an ornament, preferably with moving metal parts, such as a grandfather clock.

# FENG SHUI  2012

| SE | S | SW |
|---|---|---|
| ⚏ **5** <br> Yellow | ☲ **1** <br> White | ☷ **3** <br> Jade |
| **E** <br> ☷ **4** <br> Green | **6** <br> White | **W** <br> ☱ **8** <br> White |
| **NE** <br> **Celebration** <br> *You Bi* <br> ☲ **9** <br> Purple | **N** <br> ☵ **2** <br> Black | **NW** <br> ☰ **7** <br> Red |

**The Northeast Section**

# Northeast

## Situation

Doors, bedrooms, study rooms in the northeast section.

## Analysis

The *9 Purple You Bi Celebration Star* is in the northeast section this year. This 9 Purple Star represents wealth, promotion, romance and celebration. Its element is fire. The northeast belongs to the 8 White Zuo Fu Money Star which brings fame and wealth. Its element is earth. The 9 Purple (fire) and the 8 White (earth) Stars have a productive relationship. It makes the northeast one of the most beneficial sections in the year of the Dragon (2012). Fire provides strong support to earth element, so it becomes a celebration and wealth-making area. This combination brings renown, wealth, and excellence for money prospects. It is also good for students to pass tests and for romance. People should make frequent use of this area.

## Benefits

Beneficial for politicians, merchants, students, and married couples looking to have a baby. Prosperous for land developers and real estates investors.

## Remedy: Fire

Use fire element in this area. A possible application of fire element can be a red light bulb, a lamp with a red shade or any red decorative item. The corresponding colors of maroon, purple or fuchsia can also be used.

There is only one way to
Happiness
~ to be able to live your life

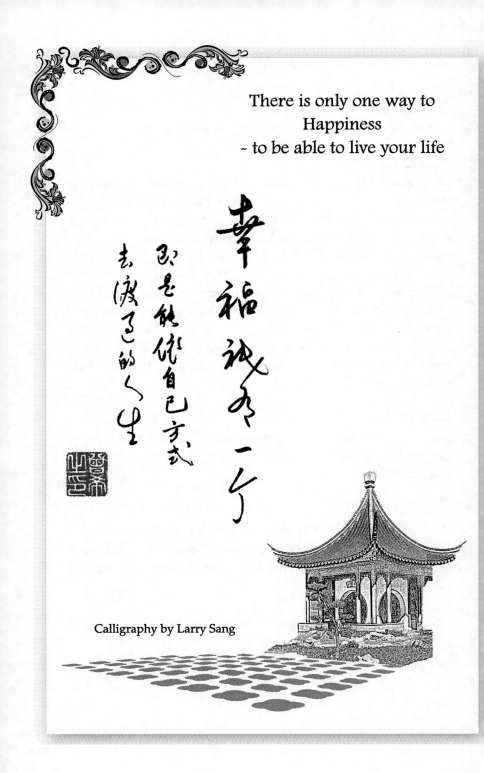

幸福就是一個

人是能依自己方式

去渡過的人生

Calligraphy by Larry Sang

# DAY SELECTION

# DAY SELECTION

## *Introduction to Day Selection*

Day Selection has been used for a long time in China. Every year, almanacs would be published giving the best days for important activities, as well as days to avoid. It is thought that a positive outcome is more likely when an activity is begun on an auspicious day. In English, we talk abut getting things off to a good start, but have no particular methodology to do this.

There are three aspects to selecting a good day: picking a day that is good for the activity, avoiding a day that is bad for the activity, and picking a day that is not bad for the person(s) involved. In the calendar pages that follow, each day will list two or three activities that are auspicious or inauspicious on that day. If you wanted to pick a date to get married, you would first look for the days that were considered good for weddings. In addition, you need to check the birth information of the bride and groom. If the bride is a Rabbit and the groom is a Rat, then you also need to avoid any days that say Bad for Rat or Bad for Rabbit, even if they are good for weddings in general.

In addition, there are some days that are not good for any important activity. Usually this is because the energy of heaven and earth is too strong or inharmonious on those days.

Day Selection is used for the first day of an activity. It does not affect a continued activity. For example, you should begin construction on a day that is good for ground breaking, but it is not a problem if the construction is continued through a day that is bad for ground breaking. The construction need not be stopped.

On the next page are definitions of the various activities included in Master Sang's Day Selection Calendar.

# CALENDAR TERMINOLOGY KEY

**Animals:**
Generally a bad day for a person born in the year of the animal listed. Even if an activity is listed as beneficial for that day, it will usually not be beneficial for that animal

**Begin Mission:**
Beginning a new position, mission, or assignment

**Burial:**
Burial

**Business:**
Trade or business

**Buy Property:**
Purchasing real estate

**Construction:**
Good or bad to begin work on buildings, roads, etc

**Contracts:**
Signing or entering into a contract, pact, or agreement

**Don't Do Important Things:**
A bad day for most activities

**Fix House:**
Reprairing the inside or outside of the house. Also for installing major appliances, such as the stove or oven

**Funeral:**
Funerals

**Grand Opening:**
Good or bad for opening a new business, restaurant, etc. Opening ceremonies for a new event

**Ground Breaking:**
Beginning construction or disturbing the earth

**Healing:**
Curing diseases, beginning a course of treatment

**Lawsuits:**
Filing a lawsuit or going to court

**Movings:**
Moving or changing residences

**Planting:**
Gardening or planting

**Prayer:**
Praying for blessings or happiness

**School:**
Admissions into a new school

**Travel:**
Going out or beginning a trip

**Wedding:**
Marriage ceremonies or becoming engaged to be married

**Worship:**
Rituals, rites, ceremonies, offering sacrifices, or honoring ancestors or the dead

| S | M | T | W | T | F | S |
|---|---|---|---|---|---|---|
| 1 | 2 | 3 | 4 | 5 | 6 | 7 |
| 8 | 9 | 10 | 11 | 12 | 13 | 14 |
| 15 | 16 | 17 | 18 | 19 | 20 | 21 |
| 22 | 23 | 24 | 25 | 26 | 27 | 28 |
| 29 | 30 | 31 | | | | |

# *January 2012*

*Unfavorable for:*

| Date | | Unfavorable for: |
|---|---|---|
| **Sun 1** | ⊖ **DON'T DO IMPORTANT THINGS** ⊖ | *Rabbit* |
| **Mon 2** | **Good for:** grand opening, school, fix house<br>*Bad for: ground breaking, lawsuit* | *Dragon* |
| **Tue 3** | ⊖ **DON'T DO IMPORTANT THINGS** ⊖ | *Snake* |
| **Wed 4** | **Good for:** prayer, planting, worship<br>*Bad for: grand opening, wedding* | *Horse* |
| **Thu 5** | **Good for:** grand opening, ground breaking, wedding | *Sheep* |
| **Fri 6** | ⊖ **DON'T DO IMPORTANT THINGS** ⊖ | *Monkey* |
| **Sat 7** | **Good for:** prayer, worship<br>*Bad for: grand opening, ground breaking, wedding* | *Rooster* |
| **Sun 8** | **Good for:** worship<br>*Bad for: contracts, burial, begin mission* | *Dog* |
| **Mon 9** | **Good for:** contracts, fix house, wedding | *Pig* |
| **Tue 10** | **Good for:** grand opening, ground breaking, wedding | *Rat* |
| **Wed 11** | ⊖ **DON'T DO IMPORTANT THINGS** ⊖ | *Ox* |
| **Thu 12** | **Good for:** worship<br>*Bad for: grand opening, lawsuits, wedding* | *Tiger* |
| **Fri 13** | ⊖ **DON'T DO IMPORTANT THINGS** ⊖ | *Rabbit* |
| **Sat 14** | **Good for:** prayer, worship<br>*Bad for: contracts, grand opening, moving* | *Dragon* |
| **Sun 15** | **Good for:** fix house, grand opening, ground breaking<br>*Bad for: lawsuits* | *Snake* |

| | | |
|---|---|---|
| **Mon** <br> **16** | **Good for:** burial, worship <br> *Bad for: moving, ground breaking* | *Horse* |
| **Tue** <br> **17** | ⊖ **DON'T DO IMPORTANT THINGS** ⊖ | *Sheep* |
| **Wed** <br> **18** | **Good for:** worship <br> *Bad for: grand opening, wedding, ground breaking* | *Monkey* |
| **Thu** <br> **19** | **Good for:** prayer, worship <br> *Bad for: burial, ground breaking* | *Rooster* |
| **Fri** <br> **20** | **Good for:** prayer, worship <br> *Bad for: contracts, wedding* | *Dog* |
| **Sat** <br> **21** | **Good for:** business, contracts, fix house <br> *Bad for: grand opening, wedding* | *Pig* |
| **Sun** <br> **22** | **Good for:** worship <br> *Bad for: moving, travel, wedding* | *Rat* |
| **Mon** <br> **23** | ⊖ **DON'T DO IMPORTANT THINGS** ⊖ | *Ox* |
| **Tue** <br> **24** | **Good for:** burial, grand opening, ground breaking <br> *Bad for: contracts, lawsuit* | *Tiger* |
| **Wed** <br> **25** | ⊖ **DON'T DO IMPORTANT THINGS** ⊖ | *Rabbit* |
| **Thu** <br> **26** | **Good for:** planting, prayer, worship <br> *Bad for: grand opening, wedding* | *Dragon* |
| **Fri** <br> **27** | **Good for:** worship <br> *Bad for: business, contracts, wedding* | *Snake* |
| **Sat** <br> **28** | **Good for:** prayer, worship <br> *Bad for: begin mission, grand opening, ground breaking* | *Horse* |
| **Sun** <br> **29** | ⊖ **DON'T DO IMPORTANT THINGS** ⊖ | *Sheep* |
| **Mon** <br> **30** | **Good for:** grand opening, ground breaking, wedding | *Monkey* |
| **Tue** <br> **31** | **Good for:** planting, prayer, worship <br> *Bad for: contracts, grand opening, wedding* | *Rooster* |

| S | M | T | W | T | F | S |
|---|---|---|---|---|---|---|
| | | | 1 | 2 | 3 | 4 |
| 5 | 6 | 7 | 8 | 9 | 10 | 11 |
| 12 | 13 | 14 | 15 | 16 | 17 | 18 |
| 19 | 20 | 21 | 22 | 23 | 24 | 25 |
| 26 | 27 | 28 | 29 | | | |

# February 2012

*Unfavorable for:*

| | | |
|---|---|---|
| **Wed**<br>**1** | **Good for:** worship<br>*Bad for: moving, wedding* | *Dog* |
| **Thu**<br>**2** | **Good for:** business, contracts<br>*Bad for: planting* | *Pig* |
| **Fri**<br>**3** | **Good for:** prayer, worship, contracts | *Rat* |
| **Sat**<br>**4** | ⊖ **DON'T DO IMPORTANT THINGS** ⊖ | *Ox* |
| **Sun**<br>**5** | ⊖ **DON'T DO IMPORTANT THINGS** ⊖ | *Tiger* |
| **Mon**<br>**6** | ⊖ **DON'T DO IMPORTANT THINGS** ⊖ | *Rabbit* |
| **Tue**<br>**7** | ⊖ **DON'T DO IMPORTANT THINGS** ⊖ | *Dragon* |
| **Wed**<br>**8** | **Good for:** wedding, contracts<br>*Bad for: grand opening, burial* | *Snake* |
| **Thu**<br>**9** | **Good for:** healing, wedding, business<br>*Bad for: ground breaking* | *Horse* |
| **Fri**<br>**10** | **Good for:** worship, business, ground breaking<br>*Bad for: travel, wedding* | *Sheep* |
| **Sat**<br>**11** | **Good for:** begin mission, school, travel<br>*Bad for: burial, wedding* | *Monkey* |
| **Sun**<br>**12** | **Good for:** travel, healing, burial<br>*Bad for: begin mission, moving* | *Rooster* |
| **Mon**<br>**13** | **Good for:** grand opening, business, worship<br>*Bad for: fix house, moving* | *Dog* |
| **Tue**<br>**14** | **Good for:** prayer, worship | *Pig* |

| | | |
|---|---|---|
| **Wed**<br>**15** | **Good for:** business, contracts<br>*Bad for: ground breaking, burial* | *Rat* |
| **Thu**<br>**16** | **Good for:** worship, prayer, wedding<br>*Bad for: grand opening, travel* | *Ox* |
| **Fri**<br>**17** | ⊖ **DON'T DO IMPORTANT THINGS** ⊖ | *Tiger* |
| **Sat**<br>**18** | ⊖ **DON'T DO IMPORTANT THINGS** ⊖ | *Rabbit* |
| **Sun**<br>**19** | ⊖ **DON'T DO IMPORTANT THINGS** ⊖ | *Dragon* |
| **Mon**<br>**20** | **Good for:** contracts, wedding, prayer<br>*Bad for: construction, fix house* | *Snake* |
| **Tue**<br>**21** | **Good for:** wedding, business, begin mission<br>*Bad for: burial, healing* | *Horse* |
| **Wed**<br>**22** | **Good for:** prayer, worship, burial<br>*Bad for: moving, travel* | *Sheep* |
| **Thu**<br>**23** | **Good for:** travel, begin mission<br>*Bad for: wedding, ground breaking* | *Monkey* |
| **Fri**<br>**24** | **Good for:** construction, healing<br>*Bad for: begin mission, moving* | *Rooster* |
| **Sat**<br>**25** | **Good for:** grand opening, business<br>*Bad for: planting, school* | *Dog* |
| **Sun**<br>**26** | **Good for:** prayer, worship | *Pig* |
| **Mon**<br>**27** | **Good for:** business, contracts, wedding<br>*Bad for: burial, construction* | *Rat* |
| **Tue**<br>**28** | **Good for:** wedding, worship<br>*Bad for: grand opening* | *Ox* |
| **Wed**<br>**29** | **Good for:** prayer, worship | *Tiger* |

# March 2012

*Unfavorable for:*

| Date | | |
|---|---|---|
| **Thu 1** | ⊖ **DON'T DO IMPORTANT THINGS** ⊖ | *Rabbit* |
| **Fri 2** | ⊖ **DON'T DO IMPORTANT THINGS** ⊖ | *Dragon* |
| **Sat 3** | **Good for:** planting, worship | *Snake* |
| **Sun 4** | **Good for:** begin mission, wedding, business<br>*Bad for: ground breaking, burial* | *Horse* |
| **Mon 5** | **Good for:** wedding, contracts, healing<br>*Bad for: fix house, burial* | *Sheep* |
| **Tue 6** | **Good for:** worship, prayer, burial<br>*Bad for: moving, planting* | *Monkey* |
| **Wed 7** | **Good for:** travel, begin mission<br>*Bad for: wedding, construction* | *Rooster* |
| **Thu 8** | **Good for:** construction, travel | *Dog* |
| **Fri 9** | **Good for:** business, wedding, worship<br>*Bad for: healing, fix house* | *Pig* |
| **Sat 10** | **Good for:** prayer, worship | *Rat* |
| **Sun 11** | **Good for:** business, contracts<br>*Bad for: planting, ground breaking* | *Ox* |
| **Mon 12** | **Good for:** wedding, prayer, contracts<br>*Bad for: grand opening, moving* | *Tiger* |
| **Tue 13** | ⊖ **DON'T DO IMPORTANT THINGS** ⊖ | *Rabbit* |
| **Wed 14** | ⊖ **DON'T DO IMPORTANT THINGS** ⊖ | *Dragon* |
| **Thu 15** | **Good for:** grand opening, school, healing<br>*Bad for: lawsuit, construction* | *Snake* |

| Day | Description | Zodiac |
|---|---|---|
| **Fri** **16** | **Good for:** contracts, wedding, business <br> *Bad for: burial, ground breaking* | *Horse* |
| **Sat** **17** | **Good for:** begin mission, contracts, wedding <br> *Bad for: grand opening, ground breaking* | *Sheep* |
| **Sun** **18** | **Good for:** worship, burial, prayer <br> *Bad for: moving, wedding* | *Monkey* |
| **Mon** **19** | ⊖ **DON'T DO IMPORTANT THINGS** ⊖ | *Rooster* |
| **Tue** **20** | **Good for:** construction, travel <br> *Bad for: begin mission, grand opening* | *Dog* |
| **Wed** **21** | **Good for:** grand opening, wedding, business <br> *Bad for: healing, fix house* | *Pig* |
| **Thu** **22** | **Good for:** prayer, worship | *Rat* |
| **Fri** **23** | **Good for:** business, contracts <br> *Bad for: planting, construction* | *Ox* |
| **Sat** **24** | **Good for:** contracts, wedding <br> *Bad for: grand opening, business, moving* | *Tiger* |
| **Sun** **25** | ⊖ **DON'T DO IMPORTANT THINGS** ⊖ | *Rabbit* |
| **Mon** **26** | ⊖ **DON'T DO IMPORTANT THINGS** ⊖ | *Dragon* |
| **Tue** **27** | **Good for:** worship, school, grand opening <br> *Bad for: moving, construction* | *Snake* |
| **Wed** **28** | **Good for:** contracts, wedding <br> *Bad for: ground breaking, grand opening* | *Horse* |
| **Thu** **29** | **Good for:** business, wedding <br> *Bad for: burial, fix house* | *Sheep* |
| **Fri** **30** | **Good for:** worship, prayer | *Monkey* |
| **Sat** **31** | **Good for:** travel, begin mission <br> *Bad for: wedding, ground breaking* | *Rooster* |

| S | M | T | W | T | F | S |
|---|---|---|---|---|---|---|
| 1 | 2 | 3 | 4 | 5 | 6 | 7 |
| 8 | 9 | 10 | 11 | 12 | 13 | 14 |
| 15 | 16 | 17 | 18 | 19 | 20 | 21 |
| 22 | 23 | 24 | 25 | 26 | 27 | 28 |
| 29 | 30 | | | | | |

# April 2012

*Unfavorable for:*

| Day | | Unfavorable for |
|---|---|---|
| **Sun** **1** | **Good for:** construction, healing, travel<br>**Bad for:** *begin mission, moving* | *Dog* |
| **Mon** **2** | **Good for:** wedding, grand opening, business<br>**Bad for:** *planting, travel* | *Pig* |
| **Tue** **3** | **Good for:** worship, prayer | *Rat* |
| **Wed** **4** | **Good for:** worship, prayer, construction | *Ox* |
| **Thu** **5** | **Good for:** business, contracts<br>**Bad for:** *planting, ground breaking* | *Tiger* |
| **Fri** **6** | **Good for:** wedding, contracts<br>**Bad for:** *travel, grand opening* | *Rabbit* |
| **Sat** **7** | ⊖ **DON'T DO IMPORTANT THINGS** ⊖ | *Dragon* |
| **Sun** **8** | **Good for:** business, ground breaking | *Snake* |
| **Mon** **9** | **Good for:** grand opening, school, worship<br>**Bad for:** *lawsuit, construction* | *Horse* |
| **Tue** **10** | **Good for:** contracts, wedding<br>**Bad for:** *grand opening, burial* | *Sheep* |
| **Wed** **11** | **Good for:** wedding, business, healing<br>**Bad for:** *burial, fix house* | *Monkey* |
| **Thu** **12** | **Good for:** burial, prayer, worship | *Rooster* |
| **Fri** **13** | **Good for:** travel, begin mission, school<br>**Bad for:** *ground breaking, wedding* | *Dog* |
| **Sat** **14** | **Good for:** travel, healing<br>**Bad for:** *begin mission, grand opening* | *Pig* |
| **Sun** **15** | **Good for:** wedding, grand opening, business<br>**Bad for:** *healing, fix house* | *Rat* |

| Day | Description | Zodiac |
|---|---|---|
| **Mon**<br>**16** | **Good for:** worship, prayer | *Ox* |
| **Tue**<br>**17** | **Good for:** business, contracts<br>*Bad for: planting* | *Tiger* |
| **Wed**<br>**18** | **Good for:** wedding, contracts<br>*Bad for: grand opening, travel* | *Rabbit* |
| **Thu**<br>**19** | ⊖ **DON'T DO IMPORTANT THINGS** ⊖ | *Dragon* |
| **Fri**<br>**20** | ⊖ **DON'T DO IMPORTANT THINGS** ⊖ | *Snake* |
| **Sat**<br>**21** | **Good for:** worship, school, grand opening<br>*Bad for: lawsuit, construction* | *Horse* |
| **Sun**<br>**22** | **Good for:** contracts, wedding, worship<br>*Bad for: grand opening, burial* | *Sheep* |
| **Mon**<br>**23** | **Good for:** business, wedding<br>*Bad for: fix house, burial* | *Monkey* |
| **Tue**<br>**24** | **Good for:** business, burial, worship<br>*Bad for: wedding, travel* | *Rooster* |
| **Wed**<br>**25** | **Good for:** begin mission, travel<br>*Bad for: ground breaking, planting* | *Dog* |
| **Thu**<br>**26** | **Good for:** travel, healing<br>*Bad for: grand opening, construction* | *Pig* |
| **Fri**<br>**27** | **Good for:** prayer, worship | *Rat* |
| **Sat**<br>**28** | **Good for:** prayer, worship | *Ox* |
| **Sat**<br>**29** | **Good for:** business, contracts<br>*Bad for: ground breaking, burial* | *Tiger* |
| **Mon**<br>**30** | **Good for:** wedding, contracts<br>*Bad for: grand opening, moving* | *Rabbit* |

| S | M | T | W | T | F | S |
|---|---|---|---|---|---|---|
|   |   | 1 | 2 | 3 | 4 | 5 |
| 6 | 7 | 8 | 9 | 10 | 11 | 12 |
| 13 | 14 | 15 | 16 | 17 | 18 | 19 |
| 20 | 21 | 22 | 23 | 24 | 25 | 26 |
| 27 | 28 | 29 | 30 | 31 |   |   |

# May 2012

*Unfavorable for:*

| Day | | Unfavorable for: |
|---|---|---|
| **Tue 1** | ⊖ **DON'T DO IMPORTANT THINGS** ⊖ | *Dragon* |
| **Wed 2** | **Good for:** prayer, worship | *Snake* |
| **Thu 3** | **Good for:** grand opening, school, worship <br> *Bad for: moving, travel* | *Horse* |
| **Fri 4** | ⊖ **DON'T DO IMPORTANT THINGS** ⊖ | *Sheep* |
| **Sat 5** | **Good for:** contracts, wedding, business <br> *Bad for: burial, fix house* | *Monkey* |
| **Sun 6** | **Good for:** wedding, business, healing <br> *Bad for: burial, fix house* | *Rooster* |
| **Mon 7** | **Good for:** fix house, prayer, worship | *Dog* |
| **Tue 8** | **Good for:** travel, begin mission <br> *Bad for: ground breaking, fix house, wedding* | *Pig* |
| **Wed 9** | **Good for:** construction, prayer, moving <br> *Bad for: ground breaking* | *Rat* |
| **Thu 10** | **Good for:** grand opening, wedding <br> *Bad for: moving, healing, fix house* | *Ox* |
| **Fri 11** | **Good for:** prayer, worship | *Tiger* |
| **Sat 12** | **Good for:** business, contracts <br> *Bad for: planting* | *Rabbit* |
| **Sun 13** | ⊖ **DON'T DO IMPORTANT THINGS** ⊖ | *Dragon* |
| **Mon 14** | ⊖ **DON'T DO IMPORTANT THINGS** ⊖ | *Snake* |
| **Tue 15** | **Good for:** begin mission, business, contracts | *Horse* |

| | | |
|---|---|---|
| **Wed** **16** | **Good for:** worship, school, grand opening<br>*Bad for: lawsuit, moving* | *Sheep* |
| **Thu** **17** | **Good for:** wedding, contracts, worship<br>*Bad for: grand opening, fix house* | *Monkey* |
| **Fri** **18** | **Good for:** wedding, business<br>*Bad for: fix house, burial* | *Rooster* |
| **Sat** **19** | **Good for:** burial, prayer, worship | *Dog* |
| **Sun** **20** | **Good for:** travel, begin mission<br>*Bad for: fix house, planting* | *Pig* |
| **Mon** **21** | **Good for:** construction, travel<br>*Bad for: grand opening, moving* | *Rat* |
| **Tue** **22** | **Good for:** wedding, contracts, grand opening<br>*Bad for: travel, healing* | *Ox* |
| **Wed** **23** | **Good for:** worship, prayer | *Tiger* |
| **Thu** **24** | **Good for:** contracts, business<br>*Bad for: planting* | *Rabbit* |
| **Fri** **25** | ⊖ **DON'T DO IMPORTANT THINGS** ⊖ | *Dragon* |
| **Sat** **26** | ⊖ **DON'T DO IMPORTANT THINGS** ⊖ | *Snake* |
| **Sun** **27** | **Good for:** worship, prayer | *Horse* |
| **Mon** **28** | **Good for:** grand opening, worship, school<br>*Bad for: lawsuit, moving* | *Sheep* |
| **Tue** **29** | **Good for:** business, wedding, contracts<br>*Bad for: grand opening, fix house* | *Monkey* |
| **Wed** **30** | **Good for:** wedding, healing, business<br>*Bad for: burial, fix house* | *Rooster* |
| **Thu** **31** | **Good for:** business, ground breaking, worship<br>*Bad for: moving, wedding* | *Dog* |

# June 2012

*Unfavorable for:*

| Day | | Notes | Unfavorable for: |
|---|---|---|---|
| Fri | **1** | **Good for:** travel, begin mission<br>**Bad for:** *grand opening, burial* | *Pig* |
| Sat | **2** | **Good for:** construction, travel<br>**Bad for:** *moving, begin mission* | *Rat* |
| Sun | **3** | **Good for:** grand opening, wedding, business<br>**Bad for:** *moving, planting, healing* | *Ox* |
| Mon | **4** | **Good for:** prayer, worship | *Tiger* |
| Tue | **5** | **Good for:** prayer, worship | *Rabbit* |
| Wed | **6** | ⊖ **DON'T DO IMPORTANT THINGS** ⊖ | *Dragon* |
| Thu | **7** | ⊖ **DON'T DO IMPORTANT THINGS** ⊖ | *Snake* |
| Fri | **8** | ⊖ **DON'T DO IMPORTANT THINGS** ⊖ | *Horse* |
| Sat | **9** | **Good for:** business, fix house<br>**Bad for:** *moving* | *Sheep* |
| Sun | **10** | **Good for:** prayer, school, grand opening<br>**Bad for:** *lawsuit, moving* | *Monkey* |
| Mon | **11** | **Good for:** wedding, business, contracts<br>**Bad for:** *grand opening, fix house, burial* | *Rooster* |
| Tue | **12** | **Good for:** wedding, business, healing<br>**Bad for:** *burial, fix house* | *Dog* |
| Wed | **13** | **Good for:** business, burial, worship<br>**Bad for:** *moving, travel* | *Pig* |
| Thu | **14** | **Good for:** travel, begin mission<br>**Bad for:** *fix house, grand opening* | *Rat* |
| Fri | **15** | **Good for:** construction, travel<br>**Bad for:** *begin mission, grand opening* | *Ox* |

98

| | | |
|---|---|---|
| **Sat** **16** | **Good for:** wedding, grand opening, prayer<br>*Bad for: moving, healing* | *Tiger* |
| **Sun** **17** | **Good for:** worship, prayer | *Rabbit* |
| **Mon** **18** | ⊖ **DON'T DO IMPORTANT THINGS** ⊖ | *Dragon* |
| **Tue** **19** | ⊖ **DON'T DO IMPORTANT THINGS** ⊖ | *Snake* |
| **Wed** **20** | ⊖ **DON'T DO IMPORTANT THINGS** ⊖ | *Horse* |
| **Thu** **21** | **Good for:** business, fix house | *Sheep* |
| **Fri** **22** | **Good for:** worship, school, grand opening<br>*Bad for: lawsuit, moving* | *Monkey* |
| **Sat** **23** | **Good for:** prayer, worship | *Rooster* |
| **Sun** **24** | **Good for:** wedding, business<br>*Bad for: fix house, burial* | *Dog* |
| **Mon** **25** | **Good for:** business, burial, worship<br>*Bad for: travel, moving, wedding* | *Pig* |
| **Tue** **26** | **Good for:** travel, begin mission<br>*Bad for: fix house, wedding* | *Rat* |
| **Wed** **27** | **Good for:** travel, construction<br>*Bad for: grand opening, moving* | *Ox* |
| **Thu** **28** | **Good for:** business, contracts, wedding<br>*Bad for: moving, lawsuit, fix house* | *Tiger* |
| **Fri** **29** | **Good for:** worship, prayer | *Rabbit* |
| **Sat** **30** | ⊖ **DON'T DO IMPORTANT THINGS** ⊖ | *Dragon* |

| S | M | T | W | T | F | S |
|---|---|---|---|---|---|---|
| 1 | 2 | 3 | 4 | 5 | 6 | 7 |
| 8 | 9 | 10 | 11 | 12 | 13 | 14 |
| 15 | 16 | 17 | 18 | 19 | 20 | 21 |
| 22 | 23 | 24 | 25 | 26 | 27 | 28 |
| 29 | 30 | 31 | | | | |

# *July 2012*

*Unfavorable for:*

| | | |
|---|---|---|
| **Sun** **1** | **Good for:** contracts, wedding<br>*Bad for: grand opening, moving, travel* | *Snake* |
| **Mon** **2** | ⊖ **DON'T DO IMPORTANT THINGS** ⊖ | *Horse* |
| **Tue** **3** | **Good for:** fix house, business | *Sheep* |
| **Wed** **4** | **Good for:** grand opening, healing<br>*Bad for: lawsuit, moving* | *Monkey* |
| **Thu** **5** | **Good for:** contracts, wedding, worship<br>*Bad for: grand opening, burial* | *Rooster* |
| **Fri** **6** | **Good for:** healing, wedding, business<br>*Bad for: burial, fix house* | *Dog* |
| **Sat** **7** | **Good for:** wedding, business<br>*Bad for: burial, fix house* | *Pig* |
| **Sun** **8** | **Good for:** burial, business, worship<br>*Bad for: travel, wedding, moving* | *Rat* |
| **Mon** **9** | **Good for:** travel, begin mission<br>*Bad for: fix house, grand opening* | *Ox* |
| **Tue** **10** | **Good for:** construction, healing, travel<br>*Bad for: moving, begin mission* | *Tiger* |
| **Wed** **11** | **Good for:** wedding, business, grand opening<br>*Bad for: moving, planting* | *Rabbit* |
| **Thu** **12** | ⊖ **DON'T DO IMPORTANT THINGS** ⊖ | *Dragon* |
| **Fri** **13** | **Good for:** contracts, prayer<br>*Bad for: planting, construction* | *Snake* |
| **Sat** **14** | ⊖ **DON'T DO IMPORTANT THINGS** ⊖ | *Horse* |
| **Sun** **15** | ⊖ **DON'T DO IMPORTANT THINGS** ⊖ | *Sheep* |

| Day | Activities | Zodiac |
|---|---|---|
| **Mon** **16** | **Good for:** business, fix house | *Monkey* |
| **Tue** **17** | **Good for:** worship, school, grand opening<br>*Bad for: lawsuit, moving* | *Rooster* |
| **Wed** **18** | **Good for:** contracts, wedding, worship<br>*Bad for: grand opening, burial* | *Dog* |
| **Thu** **19** | **Good for:** wedding, business<br>*Bad for: fix house, burial* | *Pig* |
| **Fri** **20** | **Good for:** prayer, worship, burial<br>*Bad for: travel, moving, wedding* | *Rat* |
| **Sat** **21** | **Good for:** worship, prayer | *Ox* |
| **Sun** **22** | **Good for:** healing, travel, construction<br>*Bad for: begin mission, grand opening, moving* | *Tiger* |
| **Mon** **23** | **Good for:** wedding, business, prayer<br>*Bad for: healing, planting* | *Rabbit* |
| **Tue** **24** | ⊖ **DON'T DO IMPORTANT THINGS** ⊖ | *Dragon* |
| **Wed** **25** | **Good for:** business, contracts<br>*Bad for: planting* | *Snake* |
| **Thu** **26** | **Good for:** wedding, contracts, worship<br>*Bad for: grand opening, business* | *Horse* |
| **Fri** **27** | ⊖ **DON'T DO IMPORTANT THINGS** ⊖ | *Sheep* |
| **Sat** **28** | **Good for:** business, begin mission, fix house | *Monkey* |
| **Sun** **29** | ⊖ **DON'T DO IMPORTANT THINGS** ⊖ | *Rooster* |
| **Mon** **30** | **Good for:** wedding, contracts, worship<br>*Bad for: grand opening, burial* | *Dog* |
| **Tue** **31** | **Good for:** healing, wedding, business<br>*Bad for: burial, fix house* | *Pig* |

# August 2012

*Unfavorable for:*

| Day | Good for / Bad for | Unfavorable for |
|---|---|---|
| **Wed 1** | **Good for:** worship, prayer, burial<br>*Bad for: wedding, moving* | *Rat* |
| **Thu 2** | **Good for:** travel, begin mission<br>*Bad for: grand opening, fix house* | *Ox* |
| **Fri 3** | **Good for:** travel, healing<br>*Bad for: grand opening, moving* | *Tiger* |
| **Sat 4** | **Good for:** worship, prayer | *Rabbit* |
| **Sun 5** | ⊖ **DON'T DO IMPORTANT THINGS** ⊖ | *Dragon* |
| **Mon 6** | **Good for:** business, contracts<br>*Bad for: planting* | *Snake* |
| **Tue 7** | **Good for:** business, contracts, worship<br>*Bad for: construction, planting* | *Horse* |
| **Wed 8** | ⊖ **DON'T DO IMPORTANT THINGS** ⊖ | *Sheep* |
| **Thu 9** | ⊖ **DON'T DO IMPORTANT THINGS** ⊖ | *Monkey* |
| **Fri 10** | **Good for:** business, fix house, ground breaking<br>*Bad for: school* | *Rooster* |
| **Sat 11** | **Good for:** grand opening, school, begin mission<br>*Bad for: lawsuit, moving* | *Dog* |
| **Sun 12** | **Good for:** contracts, wedding, worship<br>*Bad for: grand opening, burial, fix house* | *Pig* |
| **Mon 13** | **Good for:** wedding, business, healing<br>*Bad for: burial, fix house* | *Rat* |
| **Tue 14** | **Good for:** worship, business, burial<br>*Bad for: travel, wedding* | *Ox* |
| **Wed 15** | **Good for:** travel, begin mission<br>*Bad for: fix house, grand opening* | *Tiger* |

102

| | | |
|---|---|---|
| **Thu** **16** | **Good for:** construction, healing, travel<br>***Bad for:*** *grand opening, moving* | *Rabbit* |
| **Fri** **17** | ⊖ **DON'T DO IMPORTANT THINGS** ⊖ | *Dragon* |
| **Sat** **18** | ⊖ **DON'T DO IMPORTANT THINGS** ⊖ | *Snake* |
| **Sun** **19** | **Good for:** business, contracts, prayer<br>***Bad for:*** *planting* | *Horse* |
| **Mon** **20** | **Good for:** worship, wedding, contracts<br>***Bad for:*** *grand opening, business* | *Sheep* |
| **Tue** **21** | ⊖ **DON'T DO IMPORTANT THINGS** ⊖ | *Monkey* |
| **Wed** **22** | **Good for:** business, fix house<br>***Bad for:*** *moving* | *Rooster* |
| **Thu** **23** | ⊖ **DON'T DO IMPORTANT THINGS** ⊖ | *Dog* |
| **Fri** **24** | **Good for:** contracts, wedding, worship<br>***Bad for:*** *burial, grand opening* | *Pig* |
| **Sat** **25** | **Good for:** wedding, business, healing<br>***Bad for:*** *burial, fix house* | *Rat* |
| **Sun** **26** | **Good for:** worship, business, burial<br>***Bad for:*** *travel, wedding* | *Ox* |
| **Mon** **27** | **Good for:** travel, begin mission<br>***Bad for:*** *fix house, grand opening* | *Tiger* |
| **Tue** **28** | **Good for:** travel, construction<br>***Bad for:*** *begin mission, grand opening* | *Rabbit* |
| **Wed** **29** | ⊖ **DON'T DO IMPORTANT THINGS** ⊖ | *Dragon* |
| **Thu** **30** | **Good for:** worship, prayer | *Snake* |
| **Fri** **31** | **Good for:** contracts, business<br>***Bad for:*** *ground breaking, planting* | *Horse* |

# September 2012

*Unfavorable for:*

| | | |
|---|---|---|
| **Sat** **1** | **Good for:** wedding, contracts, worship<br>*Bad for: grand opening, business, moving* | *Sheep* |
| **Sun** **2** | ⊖ **DON'T DO IMPORTANT THINGS** ⊖ | *Monkey* |
| **Mon** **3** | **Good for:** business, ground breaking | *Rooster* |
| **Tue** **4** | ⊖ **DON'T DO IMPORTANT THINGS** ⊖ | *Dog* |
| **Wed** **5** | **Good for:** contracts, wedding, worship<br>*Bad for: burial, fix house* | *Pig* |
| **Thu** **6** | **Good for:** wedding, business, healing<br>*Bad for: burial, fix house* | *Rat* |
| **Fri** **7** | **Good for:** healing, wedding, business<br>*Bad for: fix house, ground breaking* | *Ox* |
| **Sat** **8** | **Good for:** worship, prayer, burial<br>*Bad for: moving, travel* | *Tiger* |
| **Sun** **9** | **Good for:** travel, begin mission<br>*Bad for: fix house, construction* | *Rabbit* |
| **Mon** **10** | ⊖ **DON'T DO IMPORTANT THINGS** ⊖ | *Dragon* |
| **Tue** **11** | **Good for:** grand opening, wedding, business<br>*Bad for: fix house, healing* | *Snake* |
| **Wed** **12** | **Good for:** worship, prayer | *Horse* |
| **Thu** **13** | **Good for:** business, contracts<br>*Bad for: fix house, burial* | *Sheep* |
| **Fri** **14** | **Good for:** worship, prayer | *Monkey* |
| **Sat** **15** | ⊖ **DON'T DO IMPORTANT THINGS** ⊖ | *Rooster* |

104

| Day | Activities | Zodiac |
|---|---|---|
| **Sun** **16** | **Good for:** fix house, business <br> *Bad for: travel, moving* | *Dog* |
| **Mon** **17** | **Good for:** worship, school, healing <br> *Bad for: lawsuit, moving* | *Pig* |
| **Tue** **18** | **Good for:** wedding, contracts <br> *Bad for: burial, ground breaking* | *Rat* |
| **Wed** **19** | **Good for:** business, wedding, healing <br> *Bad for: fix house, burial* | *Ox* |
| **Thu** **20** | **Good for:** business, worship, burial <br> *Bad for: moving, travel, wedding* | *Tiger* |
| **Fri** **21** | **Good for:** begin mission, worship <br> *Bad for: ground breaking, construction* | *Rabbit* |
| **Sat** **22** | ⊖ **DON'T DO IMPORTANT THINGS** ⊖ | *Dragon* |
| **Sun** **23** | **Good for:** wedding, business, worship <br> *Bad for: fix house, moving* | *Snake* |
| **Mon** **24** | **Good for:** prayer, worship | *Horse* |
| **Tue** **25** | **Good for:** business, contracts, grand opening <br> *Bad for: construction* | *Sheep* |
| **Wed** **26** | **Good for:** wedding, contracts, worship <br> *Bad for: grand opening, moving* | *Monkey* |
| **Thu** **27** | ⊖ **DON'T DO IMPORTANT THINGS** ⊖ | *Rooster* |
| **Fri** **28** | **Good for:** contracts, begin mission, fix house <br> *Bad for: travel* | *Dog* |
| **Sat** **29** | **Good for:** worship, school, grand opening <br> *Bad for: lawsuit* | *Pig* |
| **Sun** **30** | **Good for:** worship, wedding, contracts <br> *Bad for: grand opening, burial* | *Rat* |

| S | M | T | W | T | F | S |
|---|---|---|---|---|---|---|
|   | 1 | 2 | 3 | 4 | 5 | 6 |
| 7 | 8 | 9 | 10 | 11 | 12 | 13 |
| 14 | 15 | 16 | 17 | 18 | 19 | 20 |
| 21 | 22 | 23 | 24 | 25 | 26 | 27 |
| 28 | 29 | 30 | 31 |   |   |   |

# *October 2012*

*Unfavorable for:*

| Day | | Unfavorable for: |
|---|---|---|
| **Mon** **1** | **Good for:** healing, wedding, business  *Bad for: burial, fix house* | *Ox* |
| **Tue** **2** | **Good for:** prayer, burial, worship | *Tiger* |
| **Wed** **3** | **Good for:** travel, begin mission  *Bad for: wedding, burial* | *Rabbit* |
| **Thu** **4** | ⊖ **DON'T DO IMPORTANT THINGS** ⊖ | *Dragon* |
| **Fri** **5** | **Good for:** grand opening, wedding, business  *Bad for: healing, moving* | *Snake* |
| **Sat** **6** | **Good for:** prayer, worship | *Horse* |
| **Sun** **7** | **Good for:** business, contracts  *Bad for: planting, construction* | *Sheep* |
| **Mon** **8** | **Good for:** business, contracts  *Bad for: fix house, planting* | *Monkey* |
| **Tue** **9** | ⊖ **DON'T DO IMPORTANT THINGS** ⊖ | *Rooster* |
| **Wed** **10** | ⊖ **DON'T DO IMPORTANT THINGS** ⊖ | *Dog* |
| **Thu** **11** | **Good for:** business, fix house, grand opening  *Bad for: travel, moving* | *Pig* |
| **Fri** **12** | **Good for:** worship, prayer | *Rat* |
| **Sat** **13** | **Good for:** wedding, contracts, worship  *Bad for: ground breaking, grand opening* | *Ox* |
| **Sun** **14** | **Good for:** wedding, healing, business  *Bad for: burial, fix house* | *Tiger* |
| **Mon** **15** | **Good for:** prayer, worship, burial  *Bad for: moving, travel* | *Rabbit* |

| | | |
|---|---|---|
| Tue<br>**16** | ⊖ **DON'T DO IMPORTANT THINGS** ⊖ | *Dragon* |
| Wed<br>**17** | ⊖ **DON'T DO IMPORTANT THINGS** ⊖ | *Snake* |
| Thu<br>**18** | **Good for:** grand opening, worship, busines<br>*Bad for: moving, planting* | *Horse* |
| Fri<br>**19** | **Good for:** prayer, worship | *Sheep* |
| Sat<br>**20** | **Good for:** business, contracts<br>*Bad for: construction, fix house* | *Monkey* |
| Sun<br>**21** | **Good for:** wedding, contracts, worship<br>*Bad for: business, grand opening* | *Rooster* |
| Mon<br>**22** | ⊖ **DON'T DO IMPORTANT THINGS** ⊖ | *Dog* |
| Tue<br>**23** | **Good for:** business, fix house<br>*Bad for: travel, moving* | *Pig* |
| Wed<br>**24** | **Good for:** worship, school, grand opening<br>*Bad for: lawsuit, construction* | *Rat* |
| Thu<br>**25** | **Good for:** contracts, wedding, worship<br>*Bad for: grand opening, burial* | *Ox* |
| Fri<br>**26** | **Good for:** contracts, wedding, healing<br>*Bad for: burial, fix house* | *Tiger* |
| Sat<br>**27** | **Good for:** business, burial<br>*Bad for: moving* | *Rabbit* |
| Sun<br>**28** | ⊖ **DON'T DO IMPORTANT THINGS** ⊖ | *Dragon* |
| Mon<br>**29** | **Good for:** travel, school<br>*Bad for: begin mission, ground breaking* | *Snake* |
| Tue<br>**30** | **Good for:** business, worship, wedding<br>*Bad for: moving, healing* | *Horse* |
| Wed<br>**31** | **Good for:** prayer, worship | *Sheep* |

# November 2012

*Unfavorable for:*

| Day | | Details | Unfavorable for: |
|---|---|---|---|
| Thu | **1** | **Good for:** business, contracts / ***Bad for:*** *construction, planting* | *Monkey* |
| Fri | **2** | **Good for:** wedding, contracts, worship / ***Bad for:*** *grand opening, moving* | *Rooster* |
| Sat | **3** | ⊖ **DON'T DO IMPORTANT THINGS** ⊖ | *Dog* |
| Sun | **4** | **Good for:** business, fix house / ***Bad for:*** *travel, moving* | *Pig* |
| Mon | **5** | **Good for:** school, grand opening, healing / ***Bad for:*** *lawsuit, moving* | *Rat* |
| Tue | **6** | ⊖ **DON'T DO IMPORTANT THINGS** ⊖ | *Ox* |
| Wed | **7** | **Good for:** contracts, wedding / ***Bad for:*** *grand opening, burial* | *Tiger* |
| Thu | **8** | ⊖ **DON'T DO IMPORTANT THINGS** ⊖ | *Rabbit* |
| Fri | **9** | ⊖ **DON'T DO IMPORTANT THINGS** ⊖ | *Dragon* |
| Sat | **10** | **Good for:** travel, begin mission / ***Bad for:*** *fix house, ground breaking* | *Snake* |
| Sun | **11** | **Good for:** construction, travel / ***Bad for:*** *ground breaking, begin mission, moving* | *Horse* |
| Mon | **12** | **Good for:** grand opening, wedding, business / ***Bad for:*** *burial, fix house* | *Sheep* |
| Tue | **13** | **Good for:** worship, prayer | *Monkey* |
| Wed | **14** | **Good for:** business, contracts, worship / ***Bad for:*** *planting* | *Rooster* |
| Thu | **15** | **Good for:** contracts, wedding, worship / ***Bad for:*** *business, grand opening* | *Dog* |

| | | |
|---|---|---|
| **Fri**<br>**16** | ⊖ **DON'T DO IMPORTANT THINGS** ⊖ | *Pig* |
| **Sat**<br>**17** | **Good for:** business, fix house<br>*Bad for: travel, construction* | *Rat* |
| **Sun**<br>**18** | **Good for:** worship, school, grand opening<br>*Bad for: lawsuit, moving* | *Ox* |
| **Mon**<br>**19** | **Good for:** contracts, wedding<br>*Bad for: grand opening, burial* | *Tiger* |
| **Tue**<br>**20** | **Good for:** healing, wedding, business<br>*Bad for: burial, fix house* | *Rabbit* |
| **Wed**<br>**21** | ⊖ **DON'T DO IMPORTANT THINGS** ⊖ | *Dragon* |
| **Thu**<br>**22** | **Good for:** travel, begin mission<br>*Bad for: fix house, wedding* | *Snake* |
| **Fri**<br>**23** | **Good for:** construction, travel, healing<br>*Bad for: begin mission, grand opening* | *Horse* |
| **Sat**<br>**24** | **Good for:** grand opening, wedding, prayer<br>*Bad for: moving, planting* | *Sheep* |
| **Sun**<br>**25** | **Good for:** prayer, worship | *Monkey* |
| **Mon**<br>**26** | **Good for:** business, contracts<br>*Bad for: planting* | *Rooster* |
| **Tue**<br>**27** | **Good for:** contracts, wedding, worship<br>*Bad for: moving, grand opening, business* | *Dog* |
| **Wed**<br>**28** | ⊖ **DON'T DO IMPORTANT THINGS** ⊖ | *Pig* |
| **Thu**<br>**29** | **Good for:** business, begin mission, fix house<br>*Bad for: construction* | *Rat* |
| **Fri**<br>**30** | **Good for:** worship, school, begin mission<br>*Bad for: lawsuit, moving* | *Ox* |

## December 2012

|  | S | M | T | W | T | F | S |
|---|---|---|---|---|---|---|---|
|  |  |  |  |  |  |  | 1 |
|  | 2 | 3 | 4 | 5 | 6 | 7 | 8 |
|  | 9 | 10 | 11 | 12 | 13 | 14 | 15 |
|  | 16 | 17 | 18 | 19 | 20 | 21 | 22 |
|  | 23 | 24 | 25 | 26 | 27 | 28 | 29 |
|  | 30 | 31 |  |  |  |  |  |

*Unfavorable for:*

| Date | | Unfavorable for |
|---|---|---|
| **Sat 1** | **Good for:** contracts, wedding, worship<br>**Bad for:** *grand opening, fix house* | *Tiger* |
| **Sun 2** | **Good for:** wedding, business<br>**Bad for:** *burial, fix house* | *Rabbit* |
| **Mon 3** | ⊖ **DON'T DO IMPORTANT THINGS** ⊖ | *Dragon* |
| **Tue 4** | **Good for:** travel, begin mission<br>**Bad for:** *grand opening, fix house* | *Snake* |
| **Wed 5** | **Good for:** healing, travel, construction<br>**Bad for:** *begin mission, ground breaking* | *Horse* |
| **Thu 6** | ⊖ **DON'T DO IMPORTANT THINGS** ⊖ | *Sheep* |
| **Fri 7** | **Good for:** grand opening, business, wedding<br>**Bad for:** *healing, fix house* | *Monkey* |
| **Sat 8** | **Good for:** prayer, worship | *Rooster* |
| **Sun 9** | **Good for:** business, contracts<br>**Bad for:** *planting, moving* | *Dog* |
| **Mon 10** | ⊖ **DON'T DO IMPORTANT THINGS** ⊖ | *Pig* |
| **Tue 11** | ⊖ **DON'T DO IMPORTANT THINGS** ⊖ | *Rat* |
| **Wed 12** | **Good for:** business, fix house, ground breaking<br>**Bad for:** *moving* | *Ox* |
| **Thu 13** | **Good for:** grand opening, healing, school<br>**Bad for:** *moving, lawsuit* | *Tiger* |
| **Fri 14** | **Good for:** contracts, wedding, worship<br>**Bad for:** *burial, fix house* | *Rabbit* |
| **Sat 15** | ⊖ **DON'T DO IMPORTANT THINGS** ⊖ | *Dragon* |

| | | |
|---|---|---|
| **Sun**<br>**16** | ⊖ **DON'T DO IMPORTANT THINGS** ⊖ | *Snake* |
| **Mon**<br>**17** | **Good for:** travel, begin mission<br>*Bad for: ground breaking, grand opening* | *Horse* |
| **Tue**<br>**18** | **Good for:** construction, travel<br>*Bad for: grand opening, begin mission* | *Sheep* |
| **Wed**<br>**19** | **Good for:** grand opening, wedding, contracts<br>*Bad for: healing, moving* | *Monkey* |
| **Thu**<br>**20** | ⊖ **DON'T DO IMPORTANT THINGS** ⊖ | *Rooster* |
| **Fri**<br>**21** | **Good for:** business, contracts<br>*Bad for: construction* | *Dog* |
| **Sat**<br>**22** | **Good for:** contracts, wedding, worship<br>*Bad for: moving, grand opening* | *Pig* |
| **Sun**<br>**23** | ⊖ **DON'T DO IMPORTANT THINGS** ⊖ | *Rat* |
| **Mon**<br>**24** | **Good for:** business, fix house, construction<br>*Bad for: travel* | *Ox* |
| **Tue**<br>**25** | **Good for:** worship, school, grand opening<br>*Bad for: lawsuit, moving* | *Tiger* |
| **Wed**<br>**26** | **Good for:** contracts, wedding, worship<br>*Bad for: grand opening, burial* | *Rabbit* |
| **Thu**<br>**27** | ⊖ **DON'T DO IMPORTANT THINGS** ⊖ | *Dragon* |
| **Fri**<br>**28** | **Good for:** prayer, worship, burial<br>*Bad for: moving, travel* | *Snake* |
| **Sat**<br>**29** | **Good for:** begin mission, travel<br>*Bad for: construction, fix house* | *Horse* |
| **Sun**<br>**30** | **Good for:** healing, construction, travel<br>*Bad for: grand opening, begin mission* | *Sheep* |
| **Mon**<br>**31** | **Good for:** contracts, business, wedding<br>*Bad for: lawsuit, healing* | *Monkey* |

| S | M | T | W | T | F | S |
|---|---|---|---|---|---|---|
|   |   | 1 | 2 | 3 | 4 | 5 |
| 6 | 7 | 8 | 9 | 10 | 11 | 12 |
| 13 | 14 | 15 | 16 | 17 | 18 | 19 |
| 20 | 21 | 22 | 23 | 24 | 25 | 26 |
| 27 | 28 | 29 | 30 | 31 |   |   |

# *January 2013*

*Unfavorable for:*

| Date | | Unfavorable for |
|------|---|---|
| **Tue** **1** | **Good for:** prayer, worship | *Rooster* |
| **Wed** **2** | ⊖ **DON'T DO IMPORTANT THINGS** ⊖ | *Dog* |
| **Thu** **3** | **Good for:** contracts, worship, wedding <br> *Bad for: grand opening, business, moving* | *Pig* |
| **Fri** **4** | ⊖ **DON'T DO IMPORTANT THINGS** ⊖ | *Rat* |
| **Sat** **5** | ⊖ **DON'T DO IMPORTANT THINGS** ⊖ | *Ox* |
| **Sun** **6** | **Good for:** business, fix house <br> *Bad for: travel* | *Tiger* |
| **Mon** **7** | **Good for:** worship, school, grand opening <br> *Bad for: moving, lawsuit* | *Rabbit* |
| **Tue** **8** | ⊖ **DON'T DO IMPORTANT THINGS** ⊖ | *Dragon* |
| **Wed** **9** | **Good for:** business, wedding, healing <br> *Bad for: burial, moving* | *Snake* |
| **Thu** **10** | **Good for:** worship, business, burial <br> *Bad for: moving, travel* | *Horse* |
| **Fri** **11** | **Good for:** travel, begin mission <br> *Bad for: fix house* | *Sheep* |
| **Sat** **12** | **Good for:** construction, travel, healing <br> *Bad for: begin mission, grand opening* | *Monkey* |
| **Sun** **13** | **Good for:** burial, wedding, grand opening <br> *Bad for: fix house, planting* | *Rooster* |
| **Mon** **14** | **Good for:** prayer, worship | *Dog* |
| **Tue** **15** | **Good for:** business, contracts <br> *Bad for: planting, healing* | *Pig* |

| Date | | Good / Bad | Zodiac |
|---|---|---|---|
| Wed | 16 | **Good for:** wedding, contracts, worship<br>*Bad for: ground breaking, business* | *Rat* |
| Thu | 17 | ⊖ **DON'T DO IMPORTANT THINGS** ⊖ | *Ox* |
| Fri | 18 | **Good for:** business, fix house<br>*Bad for: travel* | *Tiger* |
| Sat | 19 | **Good for:** prayer, worship<br>*Bad for: burial, ground breaking* | *Rabbit* |
| Sun | 20 | ⊖ **DON'T DO IMPORTANT THINGS** ⊖ | *Dragon* |
| Mon | 21 | **Good for:** wedding, business, healing<br>*Bad for: burial, fix house* | *Snake* |
| Tue | 22 | **Good for:** worship business, burial<br>*Bad for: moving, travel* | *Horse* |
| Wed | 23 | **Good for:** travel, begin mission<br>*Bad for: fix house, ground breaking* | *Sheep* |
| Thu | 24 | **Good for:** travel, healing, construction<br>*Bad for: begin mission, grand opening, moving* | *Monkey* |
| Fri | 25 | **Good for:** grand opening, business, wedding<br>*Bad for: moving, healing* | *Rooster* |
| Sat | 26 | **Good for:** prayer, worship | *Dog* |
| Sun | 27 | **Good for:** business, contracts<br>*Bad for: planting, travel* | *Pig* |
| Mon | 28 | **Good for:** prayer, wedding, contracts<br>*Bad for: moving, grand opening* | *Rat* |
| Tue | 29 | ⊖ **DON'T DO IMPORTANT THINGS** ⊖ | *Ox* |
| Wed | 30 | ⊖ **DON'T DO IMPORTANT THINGS** ⊖ | *Tiger* |
| Thu | 31 | **Good for:** grand opening, worship, healing<br>*Bad for: lawsuit, construction* | *Rabbit* |

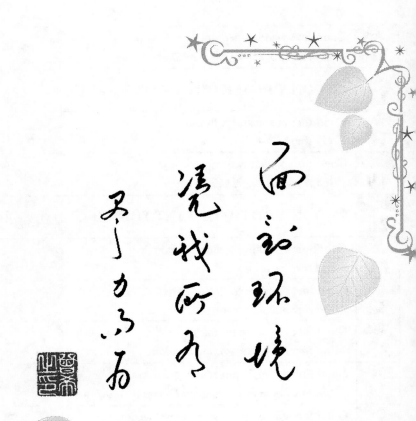

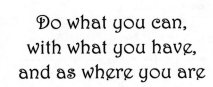

Do what you can,
with what you have,
and as where you are

Calligraphy by Larry Sang

# TEN THOUSAND YEAR CALENDAR

# TEN-THOUSAND YEAR CALENDAR

| | 1ST MONTH Ren Yin | 2ND MONTH Gui Mao | 3RD MONTH Jia Chen | 4TH MONTH Yi Si | LEAP MONTH | 5TH MONTH Bing Wu | |
|---|---|---|---|---|---|---|---|
| 1 | 1/23 Gui Wei | 2/22 Gui Chou | 3/22 Ren Wu | 4/21 Ren Zi | 5/21 Ren Wu | 6/19 Xin Hai | 1 |
| 2 | 1/24 Jia Shen | 2/23 Jia Yin | 3/23 Gui Wei | 4/22 Gui Chou | 5/22 Gui Wei | 6/20 Ren Zi | 2 |
| 3 | 1/25 Yi You | 2/24 Yi Mao | 3/24 Jia Shen | 4/23 Jia Yin | 5/23 Jia Shen | 6/21 Gui Chou | 3 |
| 4 | 1/26 Bing Xu | 2/25 Bing Chen | 3/25 Yi You | 4/24 Yi Mao | 5/24 Yi You | 6/22 Jia Yin | 4 |
| 5 | 1/27 Ding Hai | 2/26 Ding Si | 3/26 Bing Xu | 4/25 Bing Chen | 5/25 Bing Xu | 6/23 Yi Mao | 5 |
| 6 | 1/28 Wu Zi | 2/27 Wu Wu | 3/27 Ding Hai | 4/26 Ding Si | 5/26 Ding Hai | 6/24 Bing Chen | 6 |
| 7 | 1/29 Ji Chou | 2/28 Ji Wei | 3/28 Wu Zi | 4/27 Wu Wu | 5/27 Wu Zi | 6/25 Ding Si | 7 |
| 8 | 1/30 Geng Yin | 2/29 Geng Shen | 3/29 Ji Chou | 4/28 Ji Wei | 5/28 Ji Chou | 6/26 Wu Wu | 8 |
| 9 | 1/31 Xin Mao | 3/1 Xin You | 3/30 Geng Yin | 4/29 Geng Shen | 5/29 Geng Yin | 6/27 Ji Wei | 9 |
| 10 | 2/1 Ren Chen | 3/2 Ren Xu | 3/31 Xin Mao | 4/30 Xin You | 5/30 Xin Mao | 6/28 Geng Shen | 10 |
| 11 | 2/2 Gui Si | 3/3 Gui Hai | 4/1 Ren Chen | 5/1 Ren Xu | 5/31 Ren Chen | 6/29 Xin You | 11 |
| 12 | 2/3 Jia Wu | 3/4 Jia Zi | 4/2 Gui Si | 5/2 Gui Hai | 6/1 Gui Si | 6/30 Ren Xu | 12 |
| 13 | 2/4 Yi Wei | 3/5 Yi Chou | 4/3 Jia Wu | 5/3 Jia Zi | 6/2 Jia Wu | 7/1 Gui Hai | 13 |
| 14 | 2/5 Bing Shen | 3/6 Bing Yin | 4/4 Yi Wei | 5/4 Yi Chou | 6/3 Yi Wei | 7/2 Jia Zi | 14 |
| 15 | 2/6 Ding You | 3/7 Ding Mao | 4/5 Bing Shen | 5/5 Bing Yin | 6/4 Bing Shen | 7/3 Yi Chou | 15 |
| 16 | 2/7 Wu Xu | 3/8 Wu Chen | 4/6 Ding You | 5/6 Ding Mao | 6/5 Ding You | 7/4 Bing Yin | 16 |
| 17 | 2/8 Ji Hai | 3/9 Ji Si | 4/7 Wu Xu | 5/7 Wu Chen | 6/6 Wu Xu | 7/5 Ding Mao | 17 |
| 18 | 2/9 Geng Zi | 3/10 Geng Wu | 4/8 Ji Hai | 5/8 Ji Si | 6/7 Ji Hai | 7/6 Wu Chen | 18 |
| 19 | 2/10 Xin Chou | 3/11 Xin Wei | 4/9 Geng Zi | 5/9 Geng Wu | 6/8 Geng Zi | 7/7 Ji Si | 19 |
| 20 | 2/11 Ren Yin | 3/12 Ren Shen | 4/10 Xin Chou | 5/10 Xin Wei | 6/9 Xin Chou | 7/8 Geng Wu | 20 |
| 21 | 2/12 Gui Mao | 3/13 Gui You | 4/11 Ren Yin | 5/11 Ren Shen | 6/10 Ren Yin | 7/9 Xin Wei | 21 |
| 22 | 2/13 Jia Chen | 3/14 Jia Xu | 4/12 Gui Mao | 5/12 Gui You | 6/11 Gui Mao | 7/10 Ren Shen | 22 |
| 23 | 2/14 Yi Si | 3/15 Yi Hai | 4/13 Jia Chen | 5/13 Jia Xu | 6/12 Jia Chen | 7/11 Gui You | 23 |
| 24 | 2/15 Bing Wu | 3/16 Bing Zi | 4/14 Yi Si | 5/14 Yi Hai | 6/13 Yi Si | 7/12 Jia Xu | 24 |
| 25 | 2/16 Ding Wei | 3/17 Ding Chou | 4/15 Bing Wu | 5/15 Bing Zi | 6/14 Bing Wu | 7/13 Yi Hai | 25 |
| 26 | 2/17 Wu Shen | 3/18 Wu Yin | 4/16 Ding Wei | 5/16 Ding Chou | 6/15 Ding Wei | 7/14 Bing Zi | 26 |
| 27 | 2/18 Ji You | 3/19 Ji Mao | 4/17 Wu Shen | 5/17 Wu Yin | 6/16 Wu Shen | 7/15 Ding Chou | 27 |
| 28 | 2/19 Geng Xu | 3/20 Geng Chen | 4/18 Ji You | 5/18 Ji Mao | 6/17 Ji You | 7/16 Wu Yin | 28 |
| 29 | 2/20 Xin Hai | 3/21 Xin Si | 4/19 Geng Xu | 5/19 Geng Chen | 6/18 Geng Xu | 7/17 Ji Mao | 29 |
| 30 | 2/21 Ren Zi | | 4/20 Xin Hai | 5/20 Xin Si | | 7/18 Geng Shen | 30 |
| | 5 Yellow | 4 Green | 3 Jade | 2 Black | | 1 White | |
| Jie | Li Chun 2/4 6:40pm | Jing Zhi 3/5 12:28pm | Qing Ming 4/4 5:16pm | Li Xia 5/5 10:40am | | Mang Zhong 6/5 2:50pm | Jie |
| Qi | Yu Shui 2/19 2:25pm | Chun Fen 3/20 1:20pm | Gu Yu 4/20 12:25pm | Xiao Man 5/20 11:40pm | | Xia Zhi 6/21 7:45pm | Qi |

# Year: Ren Chen • 6 White  2012

| | 6TH MONTH Ding Wei | 7TH MONTH Wu Shen | 8TH MONTH Ji You | 9TH MONTH Geng Xu | 10TH MONTH Xin Hai | 11TH MONTH Ren Zi | 12TH MONTH Gui Chou | |
|---|---|---|---|---|---|---|---|---|
| 1 | 7/19 Xin Si | 8/17 Geng Xu | 9/16 Geng Chen | 10/15 Ji You | 11/14 Ji Mao | 12/13 Wu Shen | 1/12 Wu Yin | 1 |
| 2 | 7/20 Ren Wu | 8/18 Xin Hai | 9/17 Xin Si | 10/16 Geng Xu | 11/15 Geng Chen | 12/14 Ji You | 1/13 Ji Mao | 2 |
| 3 | 7/21 Gui Wei | 8/19 Ren Zi | 9/18 Ren Wu | 10/17 Xin Hai | 11/16 Xin Si | 12/15 Geng Xu | 1/14 Geng Chen | 3 |
| 4 | 7/22 Jia Shen | 8/20 Gui Chou | 9/19 Gui Wei | 10/18 Ren Zi | 11/17 Ren Wu | 12/16 Xin Hai | 1/15 Xin Si | 4 |
| 5 | 7/23 Yi You | 8/21 Jia Yin | 9/20 Jia Shen | 10/19 Gui Chou | 11/18 Gui Wei | 12/17 Ren Zi | 1/16 Ren Wu | 5 |
| 6 | 7/24 Bing Xu | 8/22 Yi Mao | 9/21 Yi You | 10/20 Jia Yin | 11/19 Jia Shen | 12/18 Gui Chou | 1/17 Gui Wei | 6 |
| 7 | 7/25 Ding Hai | 8/23 Bing Chen | 9/22 Bing Xu | 10/21 Yi Mao | 11/20 Yi You | 12/19 Jia Yin | 1/18 Jia Shen | 7 |
| 8 | 7/26 Wu Zi | 8/24 Ding Si | 9/23 Ding Hai | 10/22 Bing Chen | 11/21 Bing Xu | 12/20 Yi Mao | 1/19 Yi You | 8 |
| 9 | 7/27 Ji Chou | 8/25 Wu Wu | 9/24 Wu Zi | 10/23 Ding Si | 11/22 Ding Hai | 12/21 Bing Chen | 1/20 Bing Xu | 9 |
| 10 | 7/28 Geng Yin | 8/26 Ji Wei | 9/25 Ji Chou | 10/24 Wu Wu | 11/23 Wu Zi | 12/22 Ding Si | 1/21 Ding Hai | 10 |
| 11 | 7/29 Xin Mao | 8/27 Geng Shen | 9/26 Geng Yin | 10/25 Ji Wei | 11/24 Ji Chou | 12/23 Wu Wu | 1/22 Wu Zi | 11 |
| 12 | 7/30 Ren Chen | 8/28 Xin You | 9/27 Xin Mao | 10/26 Geng Shen | 11/25 Geng Yin | 12/24 Ji Wei | 1/23 Ji Chou | 12 |
| 13 | 7/31 Gui Si | 8/29 Ren Xu | 9/28 Ren Chen | 10/27 Xin You | 11/26 Xin Mao | 12/25 Geng Shen | 1/24 Geng Yin | 13 |
| 14 | 8/1 Jia Wu | 8/30 Gui Hai | 9/29 Gui Si | 10/28 Ren Xu | 11/27 Ren Chen | 12/26 Xin You | 1/25 Xin Mao | 14 |
| 15 | 8/2 Yi Wei | 8/31 Jia Zi | 9/30 Jia Wu | 10/29 Gui Hai | 11/28 Gui Si | 12/27 Ren Xu | 1/26 Ren Chen | 15 |
| 16 | 8/3 Bing Shen | 9/1 Yi Chou | 10/1 Yi Wei | 10/30 Jia Zi | 11/29 Jia Wu | 12/28 Gui Hai | 1/27 Gui Si | 16 |
| 17 | 8/4 Ding You | 9/2 Bing Yin | 10/2 Bing Shen | 10/31 Yi Chou | 11/30 Yi Wei | 12/29 Jia Zi | 1/28 Jia Wu | 17 |
| 18 | 8/5 Wu Xu | 9/3 Ding Mao | 10/3 Ding You | 11/1 Bing Yin | 12/1 Bing Shen | 12/30 Yi Chou | 1/29 Yi Wei | 18 |
| 19 | 8/6 Ji Hai | 9/4 Wu Chen | 10/4 Wu Xu | 11/2 Ding Mao | 12/2 Ding You | 12/31 Bing Yin | 1/30 Bing Shen | 19 |
| 20 | 8/7 Geng Zi | 9/5 Ji Si | 10/5 Ji Hai | 11/3 Wu Chen | 12/3 Wu Xu | 1/1 Ding Mao | 1/31 Ding You | 20 |
| 21 | 8/8 Xin Chou | 9/6 Geng Wu | 10/6 Geng Zi | 11/4 Ji Si | 12/4 Ji Hai | 1/2 Wu Chen | 2/1 Wu Xu | 21 |
| 22 | 8/9 Ren Yin | 9/7 Xin Wei | 10/7 Xin Chou | 11/5 Geng Wu | 12/5 Geng Zi | 1/3 Ji Si | 2/2 Ji Hai | 22 |
| 23 | 8/10 Gui Mao | 9/8 Ren Shen | 10/8 Ren Yin | 11/6 Xin Wei | 12/6 Xin Chou | 1/4 Geng Wu | 2/3 Geng Zi | 23 |
| 24 | 8/11 Jia Chen | 9/9 Gui You | 10/9 Gui Mao | 11/7 Ren Shen | 12/7 Ren Yin | 1/5 Xin Wei | 2/4 Xin Chou | 24 |
| 25 | 8/12 Yi Si | 9/10 Jia Xu | 10/10 Jia Chen | 11/8 Gui You | 12/8 Gui Mao | 1/6 Ren Shen | 2/5 Ren Yin | 25 |
| 26 | 8/13 Bing Wu | 9/11 Yi Hai | 10/11 Yi Si | 11/9 Jia Xu | 12/9 Jia Chen | 1/7 Gui You | 2/6 Gui Mao | 26 |
| 27 | 8/14 Ding Wei | 9/12 Bing Zi | 10/12 Bing Wu | 11/10 Yi Hai | 12/10 Yi Si | 1/8 Jia Xu | 2/7 Jia Chen | 27 |
| 28 | 8/15 Wu Shen | 9/13 Ding Chou | 10/13 Ding Wei | 11/11 Bing Zi | 12/11 Bing Wu | 1/9 Yi Hai | 2/8 Yi Si | 28 |
| 29 | 8/16 Ji You | 9/14 Wu Yin | 10/14 Wu Shen | 11/12 Ding Chou | 12/12 Ding Wei | 1/10 Bing Zi | 2/9 Bing Wu | 29 |
| 30 | 2/21 Ren Zi | 9/15 Ji Mao | | 11/13 Wu Yin | | 1/11 Ding Chou | | 30 |

| | 9 Purple | 8 White | 7 Red | 6 White | 5 Yellow | 4 Green | 3 Jade | |
|---|---|---|---|---|---|---|---|---|
| Jie | Xiao Shu 7/7 1:21am | Jing Zhi 8/7 11:26am | Bai Lu 9/7 2:44pm | Han Lu 10/8 6:42am | Li Dong 11/7 9:56am | Da Xue 12/7 2:32am | Xiao Han 1/5 1:16pm | Jie |
| Qi | Da Shu 7/22 6:51pm | Chun Fen 8/23 2:16am | Qiu Fen 9/23 12:18am | Shuang Jiang 10/23 9:52am | Xiao Xue 11/22 7:19am | Dong Zhi 12/21 8:16pm | Da Han 1/20 6:26am | Qi |

## The Principles of Feng Shui -Book One

After years of intensive research, experimentation, exploration and teaching of Feng Shui, Master Larry Sang put forth his accumulated knowledge and insights into this book. This book will systematically introduce Feng Shui to its readers. This book is recommended for our Beginning, Intermediate and Advanced Feng Shui classes. Available in both paperback and ebook. $18.75 US

## Sang's Luopan

The Luopan is a Chinese compass used in Feng Shui readings. It offers more information for a Feng Shui reading besides the cardinal and inter-cardinal directions. Whereas a Western compass may be used in Feng Shui, a Luopan saves several steps in calculations. The Luopan is 4 inches (10 cm) square. The Luopan is recommended for use in our Feng Shui classes and practice.                    $50.00 US

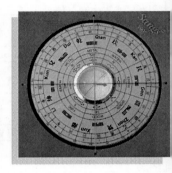

## Yi Jing for Love and Marriage

In the journey of life, we often experience times of doubt, confusion and feeling lost. What should we do when facing this type of situation? The Changing Hexagram Divination method can help by prediting what may happen. It can provide guidelines for coping with difficult situations or insight into beneficial ones. This book provides a simple method for the reader to predict the answers to their questions and to help others. Besides resolving confusion and doubt, it also provides a fun hobby for those interested in the ancient art of divination. Use this book as your consultant on Love and Marriage when the need arises!

Available in paperback and ebook. $14.75 US

### Ten-Thousand Year Calendar (1882 - 2031)

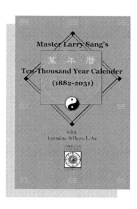

Normally printed in Chinese, but now in English, this handy reference guide is what the Chinese call the Ten-Thousand Year Calendar. This calendar contains information for 150 years, from 1882 to 2031. It gives the annual, monthly, and daily stem and branch, the annual and monthly flying star, as well as the lunar day of the month. It also gives information about the lunar and solar months, the solstices, equinoxes, and the beginning of the four seasons in the Chinese calendar. The Ten-Thousand Year Calendar is used for Feng Shui, Chinese Astrology, Day Selection, and various predictive techniques. 165 Pages.

Available in e-book only. $26.00 US

### Feng Shui Facts and Myths

This book is a collection of stories about Feng Shui and Astrology. Master Sang attempts to explain aspects of Feng Shui and Chinese Astrology, as the terms are understood or misunderstood in the West. This book will provide you with deeper information on the Chinese cultural traditions of Feng Shui and Astrology. Available in paperback and ebook.

$16.00 US

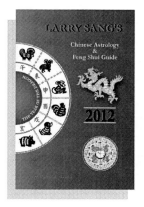

### Larry Sang's 2012 Chinese Astrology & Feng Shui Guide The Year of the Dragon

Each section explains how to determine the key piece: determining your animal sign; how to read the Feng Shui of your home; and how to read the Day Selection calendar - a valuable day by day indication of favorable and unfavorable activity. Available in paperback and ebook. $14.75 US

# COURSE CATALOG

The following is a current list of the courses available from *The American Feng Shui Institute.* Please consult our online catalog for course fees, descriptions and new additions.

## FENG SHUI

| CLASS | CLASS NAME | PREREQUISITE |
|-------|-----------|--------------|
| FS095 | Introduction to Feng Shui | |
| FS101/OL | Beginning Feng Shui & Online | - |
| FS102/OL | Intermediate Feng Shui & Online | - |
| FS201/OL | Advanced Feng Shui & Online | FS101+FS102/OL |
| FS205/OL | Advanced Sitting and Facing & Online | FS101+FS102/OL |
| FS106/OL | Additional Concepts on Sitting & Facing | FS102/OL |
| FS225 | Feng Shui Folk Beliefs | FS201 |
| FS227/OL | Professional Skills for Feng Shui Consultants | FS201 |
| FS231 | Feng Shui Yourself & Your Business | FS201 |
| FS235 | Symptoms of a House | FS201 |
| FS250 | Explanation of Advanced Feng Shui Theories | FS201 |
| FS275 | 9 Palace Grid and Pie Chart Graph Usage & Online | FS201 |
| FS280 | Advanced East West Theory | FS201 |
| FS301 | Advanced Feng Shui Case Study 1 & 2 | FS201 |
| FS303 | Advanced Feng Shui Case Study 3 & 4 + Online | FS201 |
| FS305/OL | Advanced Feng Shui Case Study 5 & Online | FS201 |
| FS306/OL | Advanced Feng Shui Case Study 6 & Online | FS201 |
| FS307/OL | Advanced Feng Shui Case Study 7 & Online | FS201 |
| FS308/OL | Advanced Feng Shui Case Study 8 & Online | FS201 |
| FS309 | Advanced Feng Shui Case Study 9 & 10 | FS201 |
| FS311 | Advanced Feng Shui Case Study 11 | FS201 |
| FS312/OL | Advanced Feng Shui Case Study 12 | FS201 |
| FS313/OL | Advanced Feng Shui Case Study 13 & Online | FS201 & AS101 |
| FS314 | Advanced Feng Shui Case Study 14 | FS201 |
| FS315 | Advanced Feng Shui Case Study 15 | FS201 |
| FS316/FS317 | Advanced Feng Shui Case Study 16 & 17 | FS201 |
| FS318/FS319 | Advanced Feng Shui Case Study 18 & 19 | FS201 |
| FS320/FS321 | Advanced Feng Shui Case Study 20 & 21 | FS201 |
| FS322/FS323 | Advanced Feng Shui Case Study 22 & 23 | FS201 & AS101 |
| FS324/FS325 | Advanced Feng Shui Case Study 24 & 25 | FS201 |
| FS326/FS327 | Advanced Feng Shui Case Study 26 & 27 | FS201 |

| FS340/OL | Secrets of the Five Ghosts | FS201 |
|---|---|---|
| FS341 | The Secrets of the "San Ban Gua" | FS201 |
| FS260/OL | Lawsuit Support & Online | FS201 & AS101 |
| FS270/OL | The Taisui, Year Breaker, Three Sha & Online | FS201 & AS101 |
| FS350/OL | Feng Shui Day Selection 1 & Online | FS201 & AS101 |
| FS351/OL | Feng Shui Day Selection 2 & Online | FS201 & FS350/OL |
| FS360/OL | Marriage and Life Partner Selection Online | FS201 & AS101 |
| FS375/OL | Introduction to Yin House Feng Shui | FS201 |

## YI JING

| YJ101 | Beginning Yi Jing Divination | AS101 |
|---|---|---|
| YJ102 | Yi Jing Coin Divination | AS101 |
| YJ103 | Plum Flower Yi Jing Calculation | AS101 |

## CHINESE ASTROLOGY

| AS101 | Stems and Branches & Online | - |
|---|---|---|
| AS102 | Four Pillars 1 & 2 (Zi Ping Ba Zi) | AS101 or AS101/OL |
| AS103 | Four Pillars 3 & 4 (Zi Ping Ba Zi) | AS102 |
| AS105 | Four Pillars 5 & 6 (Zi Ping Ba Zi) | AS103 |
| AS201A/OL | Beginning Zi Wei Dou Shu, Part 1 | AS101 |
| AS201B/OL | Beginning Zi Wei Dou Shu, Part 2 | AS201A/OL |
| AS211/OL | Intermediate Zi Wei Dou Shu | AS201B/OL |
| AS301A/OL | Advanced Zi Wei Dou Shu, Part 1 | AS211/OL |
| AS301B/OL | Advanced Zi Wei Dou Shu, Part 2 | AS201A/OL |
| AS311/OL | Zi Wei Dou Shu Case Study 1 & Online | AS301B/OL |
| AS313/OL | Zi Wei Dou Shu Case Study 3 & Online | AS301B/OL |
| AS314 | Zi Wei Dou Shu Case Study 2 & 4 | AS301B/OL |

## CHINESE ARTS

| CA101/OL | Palm & Face Reading 1 & 2 | - |
|---|---|---|
| CA102 | Palm & Face Reading 3 & 4 | CA101 or CA101/OL |
| CA103 | Palm & Face Reading for Health | - |
| CA121 | Introduction to Chinese Medicine | - |
| CA110 | Professional Face Reading | - |

## CHINESE PHILOSOPHY

| CP101 | Introduction to Daode Jing | - |
|---|---|---|
| CP102 | Feng Shui Yourself | - |

# CLASSES AT THE
# AMERICAN FENG SHUI INSTITUTE

Due to the limited seating capacity, reservations are necessary and seats are on a first come first serve basis. To reserve your seat, a $50.00 US deposit is required and is non-refundable if cancellation by student takes place less than three days before class. Please mail-in check or call us to reserve your seat with a credit card*. Balance is due on the first day of class.

*Please DO NOT e-mail credit card information as this is not a secure method*

## ONLINE CLASSES WITH THE
## AMERICAN FENG SHUI INSTITUTE FEATURE:

- Easy navigation
- Self tests at the end of each module
- A discussion board with trained Institute's Instructors
- Audio clips for pronunciation
- An online discussion board
- An instant feedback final exam

The online classes are self-paced study modules. They are segmented into four, one-week lessons that lead you at your own pace, over the four-week course. You have 60 days to complete the course work.

For more information, please see our website:
**www.amfengshui.com**

AMERICAN
FENG SHUI

7220 N. Rosemead Blvd.
Suite. 204
San Gabriel, CA 91775
Phone: (626) 571-2757
E-mail: fsinfo@amfengshui.com

INSTITUTE

## AS A STUDENT OF
## THE AMERICAN FENG SHUI INSTITUTE:

You will receive a certificate of completion from the American Feng Shui Institute, for the Beginning/Intermediate and Advanced Feng Shui Classes. Please do not confuse this certification as licensing, as there are no requirements for practitioner at this time.

As a student of the Institute, we are available to assist you with your studies. We have an online Bulletin Board for questions and answers, featuring a topic search. You will obtain access to the Bulletin Board upon completion of the Advance Feng Shui class. Due to the complexity of the courses, graduates may repeat in the classroom that you have already taken, pending available seats. Please see our online course catalog for the most current course offerings.

## CANCELLATION AND REFUND POLICY:

All institutional charges shall be returned to the registrant less a $50.00 US cancellation fee, if cancellation notice is received prior to or on the first day of instruction. Any notification of withdrawal or cancellation and any request for a refund are required to be made in writing.

Refunds shall be made within thirty (30) days of receipt of the withdrawal or cancellation notice and refund request.

The institute does not participate in the Student Tuition Recovery Fund (STRF). We are registered with the State of California. Registration means we have met certain minimum standards imposed by the state for registered schools on the basis of our written application to the state. Registration does not mean we have met all of the more extensive standards required by the state for schools that are approved to operate or license or that the state has verified the information we submitted with our registration form.

*Thank You*